And when my heart is beating
too rapidly in the dark,
I will go downstairs in a robe,
open it up to a blank page,
and try to settle on the blue lines
whatever it is that seems to be the matter.

—Billy Collins
"Journal"

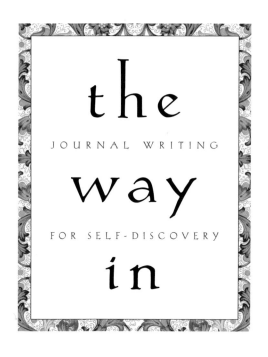

the

JOURNAL WRITING

way

FOR SELF-DISCOVERY

in

R I T A   D.   J A C O B S

Stewart, Tabori & Chang
New York

On page 1: excerpt from "Journal," from *Picnic, Lightning* by Billy Collins, © 1998. Reprinted by permission of the University of Pittsburgh Press.

Published in 2001 by
Stewart, Tabori & Chang
A division of Harry N. Abrams, Inc.
115 West 18th Street
New York, NY 10011

edited by MARISA BULZONE
designed by NINA BARNETT
graphic production by KIM TYNER

The text of this book was set in Weiss

Library of Congress Cataloging-in-Publication Data
Jacobs, Rita D.
    The way in : journal writing for self-discovery / Rita D. Jacobs.
        p. cm.
Includes bibliographical references (p. 153).
ISBN 1-58479-065-2
    1. Diaries--Authorship. I. Title.
PN4390.J33 2001
808'.06692--dc21   00-067030

Printed in Hong Kong by C&C Offset

10 9 8 7 6 5 4 3 2 1
First Printing

To My Parents
who taught me to listen in equal
measure to my head and to my heart

❦

The many people with whom I have shared journal-writing workshops know who they are. Without them, this book would not have been written. I would also like to thank the friends who—by word, deed, and example—have made it possible for me to complete this book, especially Ellen Schonfeld, my lifelong confidant, Chet Biscardi, Ernestine Schlant Bradley, Leslie Smolan, Janet, George, and Susanna Felleman, Dick Schaap, Pat Harrison, Jim Wetzler, Renee Summer, Phyllis Pilgrim, Victoria Larea, and Deborah Szekely. Thanks to Nina Barnett, my designer, who has the talent to match her vision, and to my extraordinary editor and friend, Marisa Bulzone. Deepest thanks for seeing the book within the conversation.

CONTENTS

INTRODUCTION

*We shall not cease from exploring, and the end of all
our exploring will be to arrive where we started and know
the place for the first time.*
—T. S. Eliot

This is a book for three kinds of people:

1. ANYONE WHO HAS EVER SAID "I ALWAYS WANTED TO
   KEEP A JOURNAL, BUT..."
2. ANYONE WHO HAS EVER KEPT OR STILL KEEPS A JOURNAL
   BUT NEEDS TO BE REINVIGORATED
3. ANYONE WHO HAS ENVIED JOURNAL WRITERS BUT HAS
   ALWAYS FELT THE LACK OF SOME MYSTERIOUS ESSENTIAL
   INGREDIENT NECESSARY TO BEGIN A PERSONAL JOURNAL

I've heard a multitude of reasons people come up with to
prevent them from taking advantage of journal writing,
but the major one is they are so fearful they won't keep up
the practice that they decide not to start at all rather than
courting what they see as eventual and inevitable failure.
Faced with so many pressures to meet responsibilities,
they see writing in a personal journal as just one more
responsibility, rather than as an enlightening pleasure and

much, much more. In fact, a recent study from Southern Methodist University has demonstrated that keeping a journal and writing about the stresses in your life may prevent illness.

If there's one thing I would like to do in the following pages, it is to demonstrate that keeping a journal is rewarding, and even exhilarating, on many levels for everyone, male or female, young, middle-aged, or elderly.

The urge to write can come from anywhere—the desire to have a serious conversation with yourself, the need to sort out what seems like an overwhelming number of tasks, the urge to capture the past or pin down a current insight, the impulse to record an event or perceptions of an event, or simply the desire to create a record of life's journey. There are as many different types of journals and ways of writing in journals as there are people who keep them. Unfortunately, there are also many rationalizations for avoiding beginning a journal.

My immediate response to someone in a journal-writing class who fears failure is that there is no way to fail. A personal journal is not homework, no one will ever check to see if you've kept up with your assignments, and no one is grading you. You don't have to write every day or even create complete sentences. Grammar doesn't count, nor do transitions or logic, since no teacher or critic will ever read your journal unless you choose to share it, which you may or may not ever do.

JOURNAL MYTHS EXPLODED

1. YOU DON'T HAVE TO WRITE EVERY DAY
2. GOOD GRAMMAR IS NOT NECESSARY
3. TALENT IS OPTIONAL (ALTHOUGH THE MORE YOU WRITE THE MORE OF YOUR TALENTS YOU WILL UNDOUBTEDLY DISCOVER!)

In case you are intimidated, as many people are, by the prospect of writing every day, it is crucial to recognize that journal-writing practices are as varied and different as friendships. We have friends we speak with daily, and without that communication we would feel as though something were missing from our lives. Other friends we may not communicate with for months and then, when we do, it's as though we are simply continuing a conversation left off from the day before. A journal is whatever kind of friend you choose it to be—daily, weekly, monthly, or even yearly. Ultimately, the kind of journal you write is the one you need at that particular time.

The not-so-amazing fact is once you get started, the journal-writing process often lures you into desiring more frequent encounters. Once begun, journal writing itself sweeps away your qualms. You may even find yourself writing more often than you expected and eventually enjoying one of the great journal-writing delights and benefits—tracing the themes of your life through journals kept over the years.

No matter how often and for how long you write, your journal will become a valuable tool and a worthy companion. Like a childhood wall where every new inch was marked with a pencil, your journal will serve as a place where you can see how you've grown and also, perhaps even more importantly, be the place where you will continue to grow.

So just write—there are no rules, only rewards.

PART ONE

the journal-writing tradition

Writing is an exploration. You start from nothing
and learn as you go
—E. L. Doctorow

HUMAN BEINGS HAVE ALWAYS HAD THE NEED TO DEPICT THE progress of their lives in some form—in bardic songs, drawings, notebooks, journals, and diaries. Writing to record events or investigate private thoughts is a time-honored practice dating back, some say, to the caves at Lascaux. There are many published samples of private writing—called interchangeably journals or diaries—dating from the seventeenth century through the present day, although the term "private writing" may appear to be a misnomer for words that are now in print for all to read. And, indeed, many journals that have been reproduced for public consumption have been edited to some extent, either by the writers themselves or by later editors, so they may not always display the authentic raw musings of the writers. Nevertheless, these journals provide ideas, illumination, comfort, and a kind of voyeuristic pleasure for contemporary journal writers.

Every potential journal writer can benefit from external prompts, and browsing through other people's published journals is a surefire way to inspire your own journal writing. Not that I'm recommending modeling your journal on someone else's—a virtual impossibility unless you are writing parody—but I am suggesting that reading other people's journals can get your personal journal-writing juices flowing. Moreover, it's liberating to find that not all published journals, even and maybe especially those written by well-known writers, are finished pieces of work. After all, the modern journal writer's objective is not about refining what is on the page, but about discovering and uncovering the inner self.

> *It started for me, as it does for most girls, with one of those red leatherette five-year diaries, bolted shut by a diminutive brass lock whose ineffectual key I hid elaborately in my bedroom. A journal not only required secrecy—it was secrecy. Solitude implied scribbling. My soul poured forth. My brother, idly curious, didn't even bother to search for the little key; he coolly sprang the lock with a bent paper clip, and laughed himself silly. My first reader.*
>
> —Patricia Hampl

There has been a lot of discussion about the differences between diaries and journals. To many people, a diary is what Patricia Hampl describes—that little, treasured book where young girls write down the intimate secrets of their emerging selves and confess their prepubescent crushes, fashion crises, and other angsts. Many of us, or our sisters, had those little leatherette books with flimsy locks. I had one—given to me by an aunt on my tenth birthday—which I hid carefully under the mattress, only to have it found, of course, by my brother. But even that did not deter me. I kept writing but stopped naming the important characters in my life outright and instead gave them carefully coded initials, which made my diary feel even more secretive.

But this notion of a diary as a young girl's pastime is fairly recent (if you call almost two centuries recent). In fact, Jane Austen might have helped to perpetrate the idea of the diary/journal being a teenage girl's confidant in *Northanger Abbey* (published posthumously in 1818), where she creates the following scene between the attractive Mr. Tilney and her heroine, Catherine:

> *'I see what you think of me,' said he gravely- 'I shall make but a poor figure in your journal to-morrow.'*
>
> *'My journal !'*
>
> *'Yes, I know exactly what you will say: Friday, went to the Lower Rooms; wore my sprigged muslin robe with blue trimmings - plain black shoes - appeared to much advantage; but was strangely harassed by a queer, half-witted man, who would make me dance with him, and distressed me by his nonsense.'*
>
> *'Indeed I shall say no such thing.'*
>
> *'Shall I tell you what you ought to say?'*
>
> *'If you please.'*

'I danced with a very agreeable young man, introduced by Mr King; had a great deal of conversation with him—seems a most extraordinary genius—hope I may know more of him. That, madam, is what I wish you to say.'

'But, perhaps, I keep no journal.'

'Perhaps you are not sitting in this room, and I am not sitting by you. These are points in which a doubt is equally possible. Not keep a journal! How are your absent cousins to understand the tenour of your life in Bath without one? How are the civilities and compliments of every day to be related as they ought to be, unless noted down every evening in a journal? How are your various dresses to be remembered, and the particular state of your complexion, and curl of your hair to be described in all their diversities, without having constant recourse to a journal?—My dear madam, I am not so ignorant of young ladies' ways as you wish to believe me; it is this delightful habit of journalizing which largely contributes to form the easy style of writing for which ladies are so generally celebrated. Every body allows that the talent of writing agreeable letters is peculiarly female. Nature may have done something, but I am sure it must be essentially assisted by the practice of keeping a journal.'

Given that Jane Austen was one of the most astute and ironic chroniclers of the manners of her time, we have to realize that this exchange is fairly tongue-in-cheek. Yet this view of a diary as a young woman's means of communicating with herself, or as a place for her to store the raw materials for the letters or conversations she will later send or have is still current to some extent. In fact, I have no doubt that there are a number of one-time adolescent diary writers who may scorn keeping an adult journal because they have trouble imagining going beyond that earlier experience.

Yet there are many other, less adolescent, examples of diaries that come much closer to our current concept of journal writing. When Samuel Pepys kept his fascinating diaries beginning just after the middle of the seventeenth century, he was certainly not a teenager and his entries leave us a fairly gritty record of his daily life in England. Here's an entry from May 25, 1660:

> *I went [to accompany the King to the shore] ... with a dog that the King loved (which shit in the boat, which made us laugh and me think that a King and all that belong to him are but just as others are) ... and so got on shore when the King did, who was received by Generall Monke with all imaginable love and respect at his entrance upon the land at Dover. Infinite the Croud*

of people and the gallantry of the Horsmen, Citizens,
and Noblemen of all sorts.

Pepys records events and along the way gives his own perceptions of those events. Fortunately for the modern reader, he does so apparently without the fear of reprisals that might have been visited upon someone so forthright in that era. His diaries are filled with observations of the king and the court as well as with descriptions of the attractions of a variety of women, including his wife, and his prayer to God that he be able to pay for his lovely new "camlet cloak, with gold buttons, and a silk suit." Along the way, he surprises us while giving us insights into the social mores and somewhat bawdy gossip of his era.

Pepys is probably most well known today because he closed nearly all of his diary entries with "And so to bed," a phrase that reinforces the classic notion that the last thing you must do before retiring is write down the events of the day. Yet over the years, diary and journal writers have written at all times of the day and night, whenever the spirit moved them. As Henry David Thoreau wrote, "I put a piece of paper under my pillow, and when I could not sleep I wrote in the dark." And Thoreau, like many other journal writers, did not confine his entries merely to recording the events of the day. As he wrote in February 1842:

My Journal is that of me which would else spill over and run to waste, gleanings from the field which in action I reap. I must not live for it, but in it for the gods. They are my correspondent, to whom daily I send off this sheet postpaid.

Also in the nineteenth century, Ralph Waldo Emerson recorded daily events on the same pages where he investigated his soul and tried out some of the ideas he would include in his remarkable essays. Among the most readable and engaging of private writings, Emerson's journals are filled with acute perceptions and musings about events, transcendentalism, and life. Take this entry on the mystery of human passions:

April 12–15, 1836

In life all finding is not that thing we sought, but something else. The lover on being accepted, missed the wildest charm of the maid he dared not hope to call his own. The husband loses the wife in the cares of the household. Later, he cannot rejoice with her in the babe for by becoming a mother she ceases yet more to be a wife. With the growth of children the relations of the pair becomes yet feebler from the demands children make, until at last nothing remains of the original passion out of which all these parricidal fruits proceeded; and they die because they are superfluous.

Emerson's journals cover the breadth of human experience. He can go from writing about a visit from a friend, Margaret Fuller, who taught him German pronunciation somewhat against his will, to this entry two days later:

> *May 6, 1837*
>
> *Sad is this continual postponement of life, I refuse sympathy & intimacy with people as if in view of some better sympathy & intimacy to come. But whence & when? I am already thirtyfour years old. Already my friends & fellow workers are dying from me. Scarcely can I say that I see any new men or women approaching me; I am too old to regard fashion; too old to expect patronage of any greater or more powerful. Let me suck the sweetness of those affections & consuetudes that grow near me— that the Divine Providence offers me. These old shoes are easy to the feet.*

Except for language that is sometimes old-fashioned, Emerson's entries prove that the condition of the human spirit and heart, male or female, has not changed much over the years. They also provide wonderful examples of a journal writer who moved easily between using his journal as a witness to his daily life in terms of recording events and at the same time as a place to investigate his mind and soul.

Not all writers keep journals or diaries, but many of those who did or do, leave behind a trove of information about the private self of the public person. One of the twentieth century's most prolific diarists is Anaïs Nin, who, despite popular opinion, did not confine her entries to scandals and love affairs, although they do occupy many pages, along with some delicious gossip and many, many bouts of world-class self-absorption. Jack Kerouac also kept a diary, as did such varied writers as William Burroughs, Evelyn Waugh, Noël Coward, Joe Orton, Virginia Woolf, and Anne Morrow Lindbergh. Sylvia Plath and Katherine Mansfield kept journals, and F. Scott Fitzgerald collected his random observations in a series of notebooks, which were organized alphabetically, for example, A for anecdotes, D for descriptions of things and atmospheres, F for feelings and emotions (without girls), and G for descriptions of girls, all the way to T for titles and U for unclassified.

Arnold Bennett, the late nineteenth- and early twentieth-century novelist, used both what we might call the traditional diary mode of recording events and what might be seen as a more contemporary journal-writing mode of reflecting on events in his private writing. A good deal of his diary served as a witness to his daily life, a record for himself. On September 30, 1914, his entry was simple and to the point, its purpose mainly to keep track of his activities:

We walked home. Over 2 miles, mostly uphill and over rough ground, in 29 minutes. Profuse perspiration. Change. Bath. Dinner. Champagne. Cigar. Coffee. Bed at 10 PM and a very fairish night.

Yet, if we look at an earlier entry on January 5, 1913, after he has met with the American novelist Henry James, we can see that he is developing a character sketch for his own purposes, as he might for a character to be included in a novel:

Henry James at Pinker's. Very slow talker. Beautiful French. Expressed stupefaction when I said I knew nothing about the middle class, and said the next time he saw me he would have recovered from the stupefaction, and the discussion might proceed. Said there was too much to say about everything—and that was the thing most felt by one such as he, not entirely without er—er—er—er—perceptions. When I said I lay awake at nights sometimes thinking of the things I had left out of my novels, he said that all my stuff was crammed, and that when the stuff was crammed nothing more could be put in, and so it was all right. He spoke with feeling about his recent illness. "I have been very ill." Said he was now settled down in Cheyne Walk, and had one or two faithful dependable servants, and so on. An old man, waning, but with the persistent youthfulness that all old bachelors have.

A good many diarists or journal writers do the equivalent of "thinking out loud" on paper about what form their private writing might take. In a well-known diary entry Virginia Woolf writes about what she desires in a diary:

> *What sort of diary should I like mine to be? Something loose knit, & yet not slovenly, so elastic that it will embrace any thing, solemn, slight or beautiful that comes into my mind. I should like it to resemble some deep old desk, or capacious hold-all, in which one flings a mass of odds & ends without looking them through.*

In another entry, she is almost matter-of-fact about the events of her day as she recounts a simple trip to London, but at the same time she reveals a good deal about who she is and how she is feeling:

> *15 February 1915*
>
> *Leonard and I both went up to London this afternoon; L to the Library, & I to ramble about the West End, picking up clothes. I am really in rags. With age one's less afraid of superb shops. I swept about in Debenham's & Marshalls. Then I had tea & rambled down to Charing Cross in the dark, making up phrases & incidents to write about. Which is, I expect, the way one gets killed. I bought a ten & elevenpenny blue dress, in which I sit at this moment.*

And sixteen years later, she displays a keen ability both to depict a character and reveal herself as she uses her diary to contemplate Arnold Bennett's character much in the same way that Bennett earlier mused on Henry James's character:

Saturday 28 March (1931)

Arnold Bennett died last night; which leaves me sadder than I should have supposed. A lovable genuine man; impeded, somehow a little awkward in life; well meaning; ponderous; kindly; coarse; knowing he was coarse; dimly floundering & feeling for something else. Glutted with success; wounded in his feelings; avid; thick lipped: prosaic intolerably; rather dignified; set upon writing; yet always taken in; deluded by splendour & success; but naive; an old bore; an egotist; much at the mercy of life for all his competence; a shop keepers view of literature; yet with the rudiments, covered over with fat & prosperity & the desire for hideous Empire furniture, of sensibility. Some real understanding power as well as gigantic absorbing power.—These are the sort of things that I think by fits & starts this morning, as I sit journalising. I remember his determination to write, 1000 words daily; & how he trotted off to do it at night; & feel some sorrow that now he will never sit down and begin methodically covering his regulation number of pages in his workmanlike beautiful but dull hand. Queer how one regrets the dispersal of any body who seemed—as I say—genuine; who had direct contact with life—for he abused me; & I yet rather wished him to go on abusing me; & me abusing him. An element in life—even in mine that was so remote—taken away. This is what one minds.

THE JOURNAL WRITER AS GOSSIP

We all gossip, even if we are sometimes ashamed of our delight in telling tales about others. But we can take comfort in the fact that we are engaging in an eternal human activity, sympathetically assessed by poet Phyllis McGinley:

Gossip isn't scandal and it's not merely malicious. It's chatter about the human race by lovers of the same. Gossip is the tool of the poet, the shop-talk of the scientist, and the consolation of the housewife, wit, tycoon and intellectual. It begins in the nursery and ends when speech is past.

Journal writers particularly love to gossip—in part because what better material for a journal is there, besides self-contemplation, than observations about others and their foibles or quirks. One of the more entertaining journal-writing gossips was Noël Coward, who on many occasions revealed secrets that his companions—many of whom were quite well known—might have preferred left unspoken. Here is a delicious excerpt:

Sunday 31 August (1947)

Woke late. Breakfast-lunch with Tallulah (Bankhead), then we all went to the Riverview Place park where we went on everything and thoroughly enjoyed ourselves. We came home, had a bath and changed, then went to dine at Chez Paree in order to see Carmen Miranda. From then on the evening became a nightmare. Carmen Miranda was extremely good and after her show came to sit at our table. Tallulah was nicely thank you and proceeded to be noisy and vulgar from then on. Carmen Miranda wisely disappeared. Tallulah screamed and roared and banged the table, etc., and I wished the floor would open. From Chez Paree we drove all around Chicago to a dive where there is a trombonist, a saxophonist, a drummer and a pianist who play the latest swing and bebop, etc. The audience, mostly callow youths, became hypnotized and began to wriggle and sway and scream exactly like a revival meeting. To me, the whole thing was completely abominable. I loathed it. The heat, the violent noise and Tallulah still shrieking. From there we went on to hear Dixieland music. We were driven back into Chicago and returned to a beastly little club and given a table right under the trumpet, whereupon I walked out and came home. I am forty-seven and sane.

Especially in circumstances where gossiping unabashedly with friends might be unwise, the journal serves a very useful purpose. And for those of you who feel that the urge to gossip is unseemly at all times, I can only quote the esteemed chemist and writer Primo Levi, who once observed:

> *Anyone who has obeyed nature by transmitting a piece of gossip experiences the explosive relief that accompanies the satisfying of a primary need.*

JOURNALS IN FICTION

Journal writing has become so widely practiced and recognized over the years, especially in the twentieth century, that novelists frequently create journals for their fictional characters as a way of letting the reader understand more fully the motivations and internal landscapes of the characters. The creation and inclusion of characters' private writings in novels lets the reader feel an empathy and understanding for that character that comes from glimpsing the exposed, unadorned self. André Gide, the French Nobel Prize winner, not only kept his own journals, he had his characters keep them, too. Here's an excerpt from the journal of his character Edouard in *The Counterfeiters:*

If I were not there to make them acquainted, my morn-
ing's self would not recognize my evening's. Nothing
could be more different from me than myself...My heart
beats only out of sympathy; I live only through oth-
ers—by procuration, so to speak, and by espousals;
and I never feel myself living so intensely as when I
escape from myself to become no matter who.

In *The Great Gatsby* F. Scott Fitzgerald fills the reader in on
the mysterious Jay Gatsby's younger self by including his
boyhood notes to himself:

GENERAL RESOLVES:

No wasting time at Shafters or {a name,
   indecipherable}
No more smokeing or chewing
Bath every other day
Read one improving book or magazine per week
Save $5.00 {crossed out} $3.00 per week
Be better to parents

Oscar Wilde created two female diary-keeping characters in *The Importance of Being Earnest.* To one, Gwendolyn,
he gives this flamboyant bon mot: "I never travel without
my diary. One should always have something sensation-
al to read in the train." And to the other, Cecily, he gives

the more traditional young girl's rationale for keeping a diary: "in order to enter the wonderful secrets of my life. If I didn't write them down I should probably forget all about them."

And Martha Cooley in her 1998 novel *The Archivist* creates the entire middle section of the novel as the journal of the character Judith, who is dead at the beginning of the novel. Only through a fictionalized journal can Cooley bring the character to life on the page and have the reader compare the internal life, and perhaps the reality, of the character with the memories Judith's husband, Matthias, describes in his first-person narration. The journal here is presented as documentary evidence of a life, which is, in fact, the function it serves for many non-fiction journal writers as well.

THE JOURNAL AS WITNESS TO DAILY LIFE

Beginning a journal can be intimidating as well as exhilarating, and sometimes we need a reason or a plausible motive to begin our private writing. In his New Year's 2000 column in London's *The Independent on Sunday,* Alain de Botton, the British essayist and novelist, gives the perfect reason for keeping a diary. He announces that the millennium motivated him to begin a diary "to force myself to notice that I'm currently living the one life I'll ever have."

Ultimately, writing for and about oneself, and using the journal to find the way in, is one of the best ways both to pay attention to your life, your thoughts, and your emotions and to deepen the experience of living your life in the present moment.

When the contemporary American composer Chester Biscardi began his journal as a student in 1972, his first day's entries were about new beginnings and his music:

> *626 North Henry Street, #1*
> *Madison, Wisconsin 53703*
> *September 28, 1972*
> *3 P. M.*
>
> *. . . a day picked at random, but the beginning of a new order—personally and musically.*
>
> *11 P. M.*
> *Tonight, after writing four measures onto Tartini, I realized how my basic feeling of frustration stems from the need for sexual __and__ musical release, even though they are on different levels. Tiredness, depression and frustration can be overcome by several hours of devoted, even though painstaking, attempts at writing—or loving. And, of course, even all of this can be as much a retrogression as R4 of Tartini on some days.*

Many years later, Biscardi's journal is still a constant companion and one in which he records his varied interactions and responses to people, the weather, his own emotions and ideas, works of art, and other people's writing. In the following entry from Volume XXIX of his journals (which I'm including nearly in its entirety to illustrate the way he captures a full day), we see him reflecting on the MacDowell artists' colony, a day in Maine, his work, his life, and the journals of May Sarton:

Monday, September 21, 1998
The Inn at Two Village Squares
Ogunquit, Maine
5 P.M.

Since returning from Kennebunkport, it has been raining non-stop and promises to for the rest of the evening. I slept. Rest. The sound of the rain within the comfort of such a beautiful New England B&B is delicious.

To write clearly, evenly—like when I began this journal in '72—would make me happy. My penmanship reflects the total disarray of my energies that has been plaguing me for too many years. I am "tight"—how can I compose or make love? even beginning with myself? I hunger for "other"—"the boy" still. It's a powerful image—and maybe one by which I need to be guided, driven. Still. Finally, now, in this constant rain, I am finding peace in my thoughts, focus. In the MacDowell woods I was howling louder than the red fox. Maybe going back I can find the thread to a new sanity, a new music, a new love. And I am learning to let go of "perfection"—all moments add up to a life.

I criticize myself that I am not using the peace and quiet of MacDowell well enough—not letting me open up to discover new parts of my imagination. What a burden! No wonder I constantly get uptight when I try to work . . .

Write bigger. Write bigger?

9 P.M.

I've learned that I need this. And that I can have this— often. Long stretches of time to "vacate" and be. I've discovered _mobility_!

Rain. Fog. Wonderful. Under an umbrella and warmed by a new, blue Polartec jacket, I walk to Perkins Cove in the early evening. I skip The Marginal Way this time and follow the Shore Road. The smell of burning wood on this first day of fall reminds me of Tuscany.

I am drawn to return to that little bookstore I saw the day before when I went lobstering. The store is isolated in a clutch of shops long closed for the day. It is off season, and I am surprised to see a light still on in the second floor of the small building that is at the tip of the Cove. There is a woman there, alone. Is she waiting for me?

I know that I am looking for something and somehow the back of the store seemed to be where I needed to start. I found May Sarton's <u>Journal of Solitude</u> which was mixed in with a number of other books by New England writers. She says

'I am here alone for the first time in weeks to take up my 'real' life again at last.'

Seeing this astonishes me. I almost begin to cry because in my solitude, in the woods, I am finding nothing. Not my "real" life nor any imaginary one. Not peace and not happiness. The music is stuck in my throat, entangled in anger and frustration. I have been given a toothpick—one of those insubstantial, thin wooden ones—to carve out music from a huge hunk of unpolished marble.

'That is what is strange—that friends, even passionate love, are not my real life, unless there is time alone in which to explore and discover what is happening, or has happened.'

And later, even more remarkable to me

'I hope to break through into the rough, rocky depths, to the matrix itself. There is violence there and anger *never resolved. My need to be alone is balanced against my fear of what will happen when suddenly I enter the huge silence if I cannot find support there.'*

A kindred spirit? Or am I again looking through someone else's voice to see what I might feel? Is she a mirror, or does she take me further away from myself?

I go back to the front of the store where The Woman looks at me with both concern and understanding.

"Are you on vacation?"

"In a way. I'm a composer escaping for a couple of days from my cabin at The MacDowell Colony in Peterborough where I'm fighting with my piano."

"You must be good then if they let you in there."

"Yes, actually. I am."

I am surprised and pleased at my response, not one that I would normally give so readily if at all.

"It is so good to hear you say that."

We chat about Maine, the Hurricane restaurant next door, and I tell her that it has been my childhood dream since reading The Fountainhead to spend time on the rocky coast of Maine, living, composing, being free like Howard Roark when he plunges into the sea at the

*beginning of the novel, naked. I had always imagined
that behind him, in the cliff, built into the rock, is a
magnificent house with a glassed-in living room in
which sits a long, ebony concert Steinway overlooking
the sea. Of course, the lake into which he dives is inland
from the Massachusetts coast. But as a child the scene
was unquestionably set in Maine. And I had already
built my fantasy house.*

THE JOURNAL IN TIMES OF CRISIS

> *When I write, I can shake off all my cares.*
> *—Anne Frank*

A good deal of the private writing in journals that we have
access to today was written in moments of crisis, both personal and political. And often the two are commingled.

When Aram Saroyan's father William Saroyan fell ill,
father and son had been estranged for many years. But in
the face of his father's impending death, the younger
Saroyan began a journal that has been published as *Last
Rites: The Death of William Saroyan*, in which he burrows
within and attempts to understand and perhaps heal his
relationship with his father. His personal journey
through writing serves as a therapeutic catharsis.

In the twentieth century, the Holocaust marked a turning point in humankind's consciousness about the state of the world and our capacity for evil and survival. Anne Frank's diary is the most frequently and popularly referred to example of the kind of diary that encompasses the personal and the political. In its many entries to "Dear Kitty," the name she gave her diary, we see the anguish of a teenager trying to find out more about who she is, along with her exceptionally articulate struggle to comprehend the incomprehensible brutality of the world outside her hiding place. Although written by an admittedly extraordinary teenager, Anne Frank's entries serve to remind us that the adolescent diary does not have to be childish. These three excerpts are just a sampling of the various ways she used her diary.

June 20, 1942

Writing in a diary is a really strange experience for someone like me. Not only because I've never written anything before, but also because it seems to me that later on neither I nor anyone else will be interested in the musings of a thirteen-year-old schoolgirl. Oh well, it doesn't matter. I feel like writing, and I have an even greater need to get all kinds of things off my chest.

October 9, 1942

...Have you ever heard the term "hostages"? That's the latest punishment for saboteurs. It's the most horrible thing you can imagine. Leading citizens—innocent people—are taken prisoner to await their execution. If the Gestapo can't find the saboteur, they simply grab five hostages and line them up against the wall. You read the announcements of their death in the paper, where they're referred to as "fatal accidents..."

January 2, 1944

This morning, when I had nothing to do, I leafed through the pages of my diary and came across so many letters dealing with the subject of "Mother" in such strong terms that I was shocked. I said to myself, "Anne, is that really you talking about hate? Oh Anne, how could you?"

I continued to sit with the open book in my hand and wonder why I was filled with so much anger and hate that I had to confide it all to you. I tried to understand the Anne of last year and make apologies for her, because as long as I leave you with these accusations and don't attempt to explain what prompted them, my conscience won't be clear. I was suffering then (and still

do) from moods that kept my head under water (figu-
ratively speaking) and allowed me to see things only
from my own perspective, without calmly considering
what the others—those whom I, with my mercurial
temperament, had hurt or offended—had said, and then
acting as they would have done.

From her insights into her confrontations with the hard-
ship and cruelty of war to her attempts to understand her
mercurial behavior, she uses her diary much as someone
would use a therapist or confidant. One can only wonder
from these extraordinary entries about what kind of an
adult diarist or writer she would have become.

FINDING THE WAY IN

The British psychoanalyst and writer Adam Phillips has
said that people go into therapy when they hit a block in
telling themselves the stories of their lives. In a sense, we
are always telling ourselves our own stories—whether in
going over the day in front of us—or, most particularly,
in looking back on it—or in trying to figure out what
exactly happened in an interaction with a lover, a sibling,
a friend, or even a business associate. We explain ourselves to ourselves, but usually in passing. Too frequently, when we try to have longer encounters with ourselves,
we can, as Phillips says, get stuck.

The need to find a way in—to understand ourselves, our patterns, our eccentricities, our desires, and our whims, is a prime motivator for human beings. Combine this urge with the desire to make larger sense of our lives, to create our own order, and you have a perfect reason for keeping a journal. This is not to say that if you keep a journal, you'll never need therapy, or that you will always have the ability to make sense of yourself and your life, but you will have explored a variety of ways to tell yourself your story—as well as to sort out projects, desires, impulses, problems, creative ideas, and goals even when you might think yourself blocked or at an impasse.

The rest of this book is dedicated to providing you with some of the tools and, I hope, the incentive for beginning and continuing your own journal-writing practice—one in which you will no doubt uncover your individual and unique mysteries, surprises, and talents along the way.

PART TWO

keeping your own journal

Not ideas about the thing, but the thing itself.
—Wallace Stevens

THE SECOND AND THIRD PARTS OF THIS BOOK ARE WRITTEN
to provide you with some tools and ideas for your own
journal writing. Nothing in these pages is definitive, just
suggestive because, once begun, the process of journal
writing itself will reveal new topics and approaches and
new ways of investigating your inner and outer worlds.
Every journal is a work-in-progress and every journal
writer shares with every other journal writer the desire to
discover more about the unique attributes of his or her
self. Each journal is as unique as the person writing it.
Your journal will bear your own imprint as distinctly as
the swirls and whorls of your fingerprints. No matter
what suggestions for topics you take from others, or how
many other journals you read, your own journal can only
be written in your voice because you are writing from
the inside out.

JOURNAL OR DIARY—WHAT'S IN A NAME?

This is the only reality there is. If you can get it down on paper,
in words, notes, or color, so much the better.
    —Henry Miller

The word *journal* has come into favor in the past twenty
years, partly, I believe, to differentiate between diary
writing, which brings to mind either the daily listing of
activities or the confessions of an adolescent, and the

kind of private writing which is more reflective and not wholly determined by daily events. But, as you can see from many of the chosen excerpts from historical and contemporary diary writing, this distinction does not necessarily hold true.

Ultimately, the term you use to refer to your private writing—journal or diary—is less important than the use to which you put the process. Journal and diary writers alike write to remember, to explore and to create, to record the thrills and spills, to find comfort and solace, to explore dreams, feelings, and fantasies, to deal with relationships and practice for actual confrontations or conversations, to try on new behaviors, and to get in touch with subconscious selves. It doesn't matter what you call the process, journaling, diary writing, or private writing. What matters is that you do it.

THE DIFFERENCE BETWEEN A JOURNAL AND A MEMOIR

When you put down the good things you ought to have done, and leave out the bad things you did do—well that's memoirs.
—Will Rogers

The distinction between a journal and a memoir is a fairly easy one to make, for by definition journals are private and memoirs public. There are no external rules for journal writing because journals are written for oneself and not for others. In fact, journal writing is most satisfying and rewarding when little, if any, thought is given to what anyone else will think or say about the entries. Also, journals aren't usually written with the benefit of hindsight reshaping events. There is a sense of immediacy about a journal, and spontaneity in writing is crucial to the process. In his essay "Intellect," Ralph Waldo Emerson wrote, "Our spontaneous action is always the best." This notion is particularly important for the journal writer, who must strive to silence the internal editor and do away with self-editing and self-censoring. On the other hand, the memoir writer has to be self-conscious about reconstructing and reshaping the story, events, and emotions for the benefit of readers.

In the 1990s, there was a renewed interest in the memoir as art form. There was seemingly no end to the numbers of memoirs published by formerly abused children, recovering alcoholics, the unjustly accused, and self-confessors. Certainly some of those memoirs did make for good reading; several struck chords with the general public and wound up on the best-seller lists. But essentially these reconstructions of lives that are meant to attract the general reader point out the vast differences between the journal and the memoir.

The journal can be a promising first draft or provide exceptionally useful raw material for the memoirist, but the process of writing each is very different. This was brought home to me once years ago as I was setting out to teach a journal-writing class at Rancho La Puerta in Tecate, Mexico. I had stopped in San Diego and was visiting Sea World. Like everyone else, I was eager to see Shamu, the huge, black-and-white, acrobatic killer whale. The original Shamu had long since retired, but the current Shamu was also an extraordinary performer, answering the trainers' cues, leaping out of the water, and doing the whale equivalent of arabesques. I applauded but was disappointed at the same time. It took me a while to realize why.

The previous January I had been in Hawaii, off the coast of Maui on a whale-watching boat. Marine environmental law dictated that we could come no closer than 300 yards to a whale. So when we spotted a mother whale and her calf the appropriate distance away, we dropped anchor to watch her teach the calf to slap the water with its huge fin. It was a bit like watching a National Geographic special with our onboard marine biologist guide providing running commentary.

Suddenly, there was a commotion in the water twenty feet or so away from the bow of our boat. Out of the sea two huge, resplendent gray whales breached, arched their backs, and seemingly stood on their tails before jackknifing into the deep again. The previously articulate marine biologist could find no other word than "wow," and the rest of us were breathless with the joy of seeing the extreme power and beauty of nature revealed so mightily and so unexpectedly. After that, I have to admit, Shamu was a pale imitation.

So what does this story have to do with journals and memoirs? To my mind, the writer of a memoir is training his own personal Shamu, a powerful and exciting creature of remarkable depth, to fit a formula of sorts because the performance has to get a response from an audience. On the other hand, you as a journal writer have the opportunity to be seized, surprised, and left breathless by the unedited spontaneity of insight that can come pouring out of your very own being. Every time I experience this quality of surprising insight from writing a journal entry—be it a dialogue, a spontaneous list, or a freewriting that uncovers hidden depths or concerns—I think of those huge gray leaping whales who thrilled twelve people on a boat by giving them the chance to experience the unexpected mystery close up.

Choose a Book

Choosing the kind of book to write in is a very deliberate act for most journal writers. A great many of us relate with more than merely a visual sensitivity to books; we react to the heft and feel of them, to the expectations they harbor, to the possibilities we can create within. This goes back to our earliest experiences with the books we first wrote in—the excitement of holding the book in your hands for the first time, the titillation of making your first mark on that first page, thereby branding the book your own, and the feeling of absolute mastery in your private power to control both the rhythm and speed of filling those pages.

My own reaction to a potential journal book is intimate and visceral, and it begins before I've written a single word. I am enamored of stationery stores and bookstores with their seductive displays of gorgeous blank books. But for many years, I kept my journal in those black-and-white marbleized books I first encountered in grammar school. Part of my reason for choosing them was that they didn't intimidate me. I didn't feel as though they were too costly or too beautiful to ruin with my unedited scribblings.

I have since discovered that there are many people who

have the same fear I had—that too beautiful a book might force me to write only perfect sentences and thoughts, which would defeat the purpose of keeping a journal. Other people are infinitely braver. They choose the most beautiful and sensual books they can find from the very beginning and select the most luxurious of fountain pens. And then they plunge in and write freely. A reluctance to risk writing spontaneously in books that seem to demand perfection might say something about a lack of self-confidence or an inability to pamper oneself, but it is no indication one way or another about the kind of journal you will keep.

Moreover, it ultimately makes no difference what kind of book or pen you choose, and there is an almost certain guarantee that over time your choices will change. The goal in selecting a book is to find one that feels like a good companion at that moment, the kind of book that you look forward to opening or carrying with you. This means that some journal writers will choose plain books and others fancy books. Some will need lined books and others unlined ones. Some will write with Mont Blanc pens and others with whatever pen or pencil or crayon is at hand.

Often journal writers bring other elements into their books, and I'll talk about drawing and visual images in journals later, but I just want to mention the possibility of putting a favorite phrase or meditation in the front of the book. One of my journals has a postcard pasted on the inside cover. It reads "Forgive or Relive." I felt I had been holding onto old angers for too long when I began that journal, and this card was a very succinct reminder to me to deal with that issue in my writing. So if you have some personal reminder or inspirational quote that speaks to you or that you want to remember, put it in the front of your journal, and you will see it every time you open the book.

A Few Words About Computers

Writing on a computer is another option, one that eliminates the question of choosing the right book. With the rise in use of personal computers, and laptops especially, many journal writers are finding it more convenient to dedicate floppy disks or files to their journals. The computer is a useful tool, and if you are a proficient typist or keyboarder, you may be able to write on a computer as fluidly as you would by hand.

It's wise to be aware, though, since we do so much of our work-related writing on computers, that very often the process of putting pen to paper, especially in free-flowing journal writing, can be more conducive to reaching our uncensored depths. But try the computer in some of the following activities to see if it works for you.

Keep Everything You Write

My marbleized school books also serve another purpose. They are bound books, sewn together at the seam, so I am not as tempted to rip out a page as I might be from a spiral-bound notebook. Over the years I have learned that in journal writing, as opposed to any other kind of writing I do, there are no mistakes. All journals are works in progress, and everything you write is valuable. This is at first a difficult lesson for those of us who are dedicated to editing and revising.

As you'll see later in some of the suggested activities, what you might consider a mistake—using the wrong word, for example—can really be an insight that your subconscious is delivering to the page. Since there is no possibility of making a mistake in journal writing, you can write in pen, or with a pencil without an eraser, and there is never any reason to rip out a page.

Date Every Entry

Most diarists and journal writers date their entries, which is a logical and important way to make sure that a writer can trace ideas and emotions to past events and periods. Dating entries is crucial to helping us reflect on past events and the way the currents of our lives flow. One of the great pleasures in rereading a journal is to find out how far we've traveled emotionally and/or intellectually from an event, although at times the dates can remind us that we may be treading water in the same place for longer than we would like.

There are too, of course, journal writers who never intend to look back and those who, in fact, destroy their journals after a set period of time. I know a woman novelist who burns her journals at the end of each year. Dating entries does not serve any purpose for this kind of writer. But the impulsive destroyer of journals should take a lesson from the photographer Edward Weston, who destroyed the journals he wrote between 1920 and 1923 and later regretted his action.

There may also be other reasons for not dating a journal. In the notebooks used as sketch pads for his stories and novels, F. Scott Fitzgerald didn't date the entries, perhaps because most of them were to be used in the fiction that he hoped would be timeless. These observations, descriptions, and bits of dialogue are as effective and provocative today as when he wrote them, beginning with his college years in the adolescence of the twentieth century and continuing through the 1920s and 1930s:

> *I have asked a lot of my emotions—one hundred and twenty stories. The price was high, right up with Kipling, because there was one little drop of something,*

not blood, not a tear, not my seed, but me more inti-
mately than these, in every story, it was the extra I had.
Now it has gone and I am just like you now.

She was one of those people who would just as soon
starve in a garret with a man—if she didn't have to.

She wanted to crawl into his pocket and be safe forever.

It grows harder to write because there is much less
weather than when I was a boy and practically no men
and women at all.

Ernest Hemingway, while careful to avoid clichés in his
work, fairly revels in them in his private life, his favorite
being "Parbleu!" ("so what?"—French), and "Yes, We
Have No Bananas." Contrary to popular opinion, he is
not as tall as Thomas Wolfe, standing only six feet five
in his health belt. He is naturally clumsy with his body,
but shooting from a blind or from adequate cover, makes
a fine figure of a man. We are happy to announce that
his work will appear in future exclusively on United
States postage stamps.

He repeated to himself an old French proverb that he
had made up that morning.

"What kind of a man was he?"
"Well, he was one of those men who come in a door and
make any woman with them look guilty."

There is little that is more frustrating to a journal writer than reading journals from the past and not knowing when the entry was made. Of course, at times you will go back, reread, and perhaps not remember a person you have written about, especially if you use only a first name or initial. But if one of your goals in keeping a journal is to learn more about yourself and perhaps to trace your own development in terms of moods, emotions, and thoughts, it is important to date every entry and perhaps even to note where you were when you made it. The date and place alone can conjure up a memory, one that might or might not jibe with the journal entry that you are rereading. This practice is absolutely essential if you're keeping a travel journal or a progress or transition journal, but I suggest dating all entries.

No Taboos

Journal writers explore various parts of themselves in their journals, and private writing can only be completely effective if it is uncensored. A spontaneous journal entry can encompass the widest possible range of human emotion, thought, and imagination, everything from fantasy to anger to joy to revenge and beyond. The urge to censor or edit prevents journal writers from exploring their true selves.

Here's a journal entry made by Christina Baldwin that she

includes in a book on journal writing, *Life's Companion: Journal Writing as a Spiritual Quest:*

> *I can tell the difference between sexual and spiritual energy, even though they emanate from the same place in my body. Sexual energy wants orgasm and then is satisfied. Orgasm passes through spiritual energy like a blip on a radar screen. It is not particularly satisfying, and it's somehow not relevant. Having a lot of energy in my body is a strange sensation, both pleasurable and slightly uncomfortable. I try to convert spiritual energy to sexual energy sometimes because I know what to do with sexual energy. I know how to dissipate it.*

> *But there is some essential difference I recognize from the start of the sensation. I would have gotten myself in a lot less trouble over the years if I'd been willing to admit I knew this difference and then honored it. The reason I don't is that when I'm full of spiritual energy, I feel like the spirit wants me to do something that I'm not very good at—passing on unconditional love. I feel hokey sending "love energy" out of my body into the room—like, I'm not a saint. I don't want to be a saint. I want to play softball and go dancing, have a couple of beers. . .and I guess I want to be a spiritual conduit too because I keep meditating. The cats come in and make a purring circle next to me. They're picking up something. Love?*

This entry is a kind of meditation on the difference between the two kinds of energies, and it may, perhaps, even have been edited, since it is published. But whether edited or not, it does touch on issues that not everyone feels comfortable talking about, but which are important to feel free to explore in a journal. Sexuality is one of these issues, as are feelings about the body or the recording of troubling experiences. A journal is the place to explore aspects of your life that might be threatening to air in public. In fact, your journal is the perfect place to explore those matters or others which make you less than comfortable but which you would like to investigate further.

The Importance of Privacy

My experience of diaries is that
they always give things away.
—Graham Greene

We all have stories about journal privacy violated, ranging from the younger sibling who jimmied the lock on a first journal to the jealous lover who just could not resist reading a journal found or unearthed.

When my friend's stepson was thirteen, several months after he had moved into the newly combined household she and his father had created, she found and read his journal. Actually, *found* is not the right word. She knew he was keeping a journal, and she searched for it and located it under his bed. Unwisely, I think, given her own behavior, she tried to talk with him about what he had written about her. She thought she was being gentle and conciliatory, but he called her a bully and a thief and clammed up. He also stopped writing in his journal.

Another story about the invasion of privacy turns out more positively. My friend's husband found her journal on the kitchen table where she had left it after they had had an argument. He read it, going against one of the ground rules of their relationship. But in this case, after ranting about his hurt and outrage and listing the things that were wrong with her, he suggested that they try to work out their problems.

These kinds of violations are every journal writer's nightmare—whether the ultimate result is positive or negative—and unfortunately, journals are frequently read without the permission of the writer. But journal writers have to recognize a responsibility both to their journals and to the people around them. A journal left lying about is too tempting for most people to resist opening, and it is up to journal writers to guard the privacy of their journals.

Journals are essentially personal, and keeping them private is important. We confide our deepest and most intimate feelings and fantasies in them and use them to work out problems that we may be having with the people in our lives, both personally and professionally. Sharing a journal with others is always an option, but it should be the writer's option. Therefore, it is essential to recognize your own need for privacy and to figure out a way to keep your journal private, especially if you share your living space with others.

There are a variety of ways to do this.
1. Tell the people in your household that you are keeping a journal and that it is private. Ask that your privacy be respected. If you are open to sharing some of your journal with others, you might also suggest that if someone is curious about what you've been writing, he or she should ask if you'd be willing to share it.
2. Find a place that is yours alone—your desk, sock drawer, or car trunk—and keep your journal there.
3. Buy a small file cabinet with a lock or a lockbox and store your journals in it.

However you feel about privacy and whichever way you choose to ensure it, consider the privacy factor before you are surprised by someone reading your journal without your permission just because you've left it around. Of course, if this does happen, there is the possibility that you want it to be read. But it is wise to make sharing your journal a conscious choice.

When and Where to Write

We all have different rhythms. Some of us are larks, some owls, and others burn the candle at both ends as long as it will last. I am usually a nighttime journal writer if I'm at home, writing in bed before I shut off the light. Yet, if I'm on the road alone, I take my journal to breakfast and find that the best place and time to write. But I am not wedded to times and places. Once, on a travel-writing assignment, I found myself the only person dining alone in a rather upscale restaurant in Copenhagen. What was most embarrassing for me was that I was seated at a table for four in the middle of a room, while every banquette seat lining the room was occupied. During that meal, my journal became, as it had many times before, my companion for the evening, and I wrote extensively, sharing my perceptions of the food, the ambience, and my fantasies about the other diners.

Lots of writing experts have suggestions about where and when to write. Natalie Goldberg, author of *Writing Down the Bones: Freeing the Writer Within,* is a proponent of coffeeshop writing, which is an easy suggestion to follow given the proliferation of coffeeshops these days. The novelist

May Sarton believes that early mornings are the best times to move inward and discover the writer within.

When and where to write is obviously up to you. You know your own rhythms best. But when you're beginning to develop your journal-writing practice, it is wise to experiment with both different times of day and different places to see what works best for you. Try taking your journal to a meal, or to the dentist's waiting room, or to a park bench, or to bed. I know one man who finds the bathtub the most relaxing place in his life and there he writes, resting his journal on a board he lays across the tub. Eventually, you will either find the perfect place to write or find that there is more than one good place for you to make your journal entries.

KINDS OF JOURNALS

> *How do I know what I think till I see what I say*
> *—E. M. Forster*

There is no absolute need to create different journals for different purposes. One journal can be sufficient for every journal-writing need you have—making lists, jotting down ideas, exploring feelings, reflecting on the events of your life, recalling dreams, and sharing confidences, thoughts, and angers. In fact, it might be best to begin with one all-purpose interior monologue journal until, if ever, you develop a sense of the kinds of separate journals you might eventually want to keep. The all-purpose journal is the kind most of us keep, either faithfully or sporadically. And that one journal serves us well as a multifaceted confidant.

After a while, your writing will tell you what other kinds of journals you might want to keep—and there are as many different kinds as activities you can think of—reading, traveling, gardening, job changing, healing, dreaming. It can be rewarding and liberating to dedicate a specific journal to an event or process, knowing that it is the perfect place to turn to for that one particular area of your life. Whether you are thinking of creating a journal with a precise focus, or just wondering about different kinds of journal entries you might want to make, here are a few suggestions:

Travel Journals

The use of traveling is to regulate imagination by reality, and instead of thinking how things may be, to see them as they are.
—*Samuel Johnson*

Travel journals have a venerable history, having been kept by well-known scientists, artists, and writers, as well as by many lesser mortals. We can still get lost in the worlds discovered in Charles Darwin's *The Voyage of the Beagle*, Paul Gauguin's *Noa Noa: voyage de Tahiti*, James Boswell's *Journal of a Tour to the Hebrides*, or the intrepid nineteenth-century woman traveler Isabelle Eberhardt's *The Passionate Nomad*, which she kept as she traveled through the Middle East disguised as a man. There were several Victorian women travelers like Eberhardt who are known now for their journals depicting journeys women were not supposed to make, and then there are the journals kept by pioneer women traveling westward, some of which have been collected in *Women's Diaries of the Westward Journey* by Lillian Schlissel. Many voyagers, especially first-time travelers to exotic and even not-so-exotic places, keep journals just to remind themselves of what it was like to be where they were and to reexperience what they experienced at that particular time.

When I plan or start out on a trip, I usually buy a new journal to take with me. A new book conjures up a clean slate, as well as the idea of fresh and new adventures. I begin before I leave with plans for the trip, making notes about places I want to visit and the reasons for my choices. I also record comments that friends or guidebooks have made about these places and include some specifics as well, such as directions, opening hours and closing days of museums, and phone numbers of contacts.

But the real joy of the travel journal is to record impressions and feelings that are intense at the moment but may fade with the passage of time and the hassles of airports, train stations, customs, and baggage. Rereading a travel journal from an earlier time brings back the smells, sights, and sounds of a place. I recently reread a section of the journal that I kept on my first trip to Italy in 1983. It brought back a forgotten wild ride in very few words:

12 June 1983

Cala Purgatoria—dirt road to Porto Ercole. Sitting in a cafe with Campari y soda after a threatening frightening ride. I'm not sure I accepted how frightening it was until it was over and I felt my breath come out. Precipitous drops into the sea on steep grades—a road wide enough for one car but where two were permitted. There is no option but to pull as close to the side as possible and pray that the other car passes safely. Then it turns to dirt— bumpy, gravelly dirt. The views were spectacular, but I could not get my eyes off the road as V reminded me. I was hanging on for dear life to window and handle. At least she had the wheel!

A few years ago, I bicycled across the southern Bohemian region of the Czech Republic, and I began my travel journal with expectations for the trip, as well as lists of all the things I would need to bring to make a biking holiday possible and comfortable. The journal goes on through the plane trip and arrival, but I find that it really takes off once I begin to describe the people on the trip, my fellow travelers with all their endearing quirks. Travel journals are like travel photographs—if you only capture the monuments, years later you're looking back on picture postcards rather than on an intimately personal record. So write about the people you meet, the foods you eat, and some of the less spectacular moments on the road. Even boredom can make for an intriguing entry.

Special-Event Journals

This kind of journal can serve as a record of the preparations and feelings about an upcoming event such as a wedding, a birth, a big party; or it might be used as a journal based on the aftermath of an event.

Many people keep baby books and wedding albums, but what I am suggesting is a record of intimate thoughts along with photos or keepsakes. For example, don't just paste a photograph in a journal of this sort—make an entry alongside it. If there's a scrap of paper on which you wrote an important address or phone number, paste that in the journal and make an entry next to it.

My favorite example of a special-event keepsake journal is one that a male friend decided to keep on the birth of his daughter. His plan was to write her a long letter every year on her birthday and then give them all to her when she was eighteen and ready to go off to college (or so he hoped). Each year he pasted a photo of her in the book and wrote a letter under it. Eighteen years later he gave his daughter what is still the best birthday present I can imagine.

Planning and Progress Journals

This kind of journal can be used to track a project that evolves over time, such as a long writing assignment, the resolution of a major problem, building a house, or even developing a new workout plan or diet. The journal can help reinforce your commitment and renew your energies as well as provide a space for cheers as well as doubts and frustrations.

In 1989 I traveled for five months with the Pulitzer Prize–winning photographer Eddie Adams in order to write an annual report for the H.J. Heinz Company. Our mission was to profile families in eight locations around the world and discuss how Heinz was attentive to the needs of local markets. To keep track of the project and my life on the road, and to gather information for the annual report, I kept an extensive diary/journal. Not all of the entries were about the work, but most of them provided me with information that eventually shaped the project. Here are a few samples:

24 January 1989, Tokyo

This is it: I'm in Tokyo alone—Eddie to follow—and have arranged meetings with Heinz-Japan and the Hamana family. I'm excited but nervous. What if Japan's lacquered surfaces are truly impenetrable, and the Hamanas are ultimately polite but unwilling or unable to speak openly to a stranger? Other worry— the structure of the book is still amorphous. I'll begin with the working outline Bennett and I discussed— centering my questions around work, leisure and home life, but I have to keep reminding myself I'm still in the sponge state, absorbing all I can. The book will have to evolve.

25 January 1989, Tokyo

Mr. Ito from Heinz picked me up at 10 AM. He was supposed to be holding a copy of Time magazine, but had it in his inside pocket instead, making it impossible for me to spot him. Finally we were the last two people standing around the imperial Hotel lobby. Language may be a bigger problem than I thought. . .

16 April 1989, Harare, Zimbabwe

Caston Nyawo summed up Rhodesia's transition into independent Zimbabwe, "I was 18 and on my first trip outside Rhodesia. On the plane bound for England a white stewardess asked if she could bring me a drink. I was so shocked by the thought of a white person waiting on me that I couldn't answer. My greatest delight is that my children have only known Zimbabwe's independence. They will never have to experience that shock." The official facts: Living areas that were lily white in segregated Rhodesia are racially mixed in nine-year-old Zimbabwe, as are schools and business, and the black population has open access. . . .Why then, when I took the Nyawos for lunch at my hotel, were they the only black people present besides the waiters.

Of course, not everything in my journal made it into my finished report, but I believe that keeping a record of many seemingly extraneous things and then rereading these journals to mine them for insights made the completed annual report a much better product. Not to mention that these journals still provide me with the background story of my life on the road for five months.

Transition Journals

> *For the man who has lost his homeland,*
> *writing becomes a place to live.*
> —*Theodore Adorno*

Any change in circumstances is a made-to-order opportunity for journal writing. Whether you are starting a new job, a degree program, or moving to a new city, tracking your movements, ideas, and emotions can give you insight and understanding into your behavior and help you to sort out impressions and gain perspective on potentially overwhelming stimuli.

Often our identities come from the job we have or the position we hold in the world, be it parent, spouse, or lover. When dispossessed in some way from that identity, we tend to feel adrift in the world. Writing both about that feeling and about the moves we make to moor ourselves once again can be instrumental in the healing and renewal process and can provide a record of how we misstep and survive best.

A number of years ago, Herb Trimpe, a comic book artist, was downsized at the age of 56 when the company he worked for went bankrupt. He decided to reinvent himself and become a seventh-grade art teacher. Excerpts from his transition journal were published in the *New York Times* on January 9, 2000. Here are a few selected entries:

> *May 27: Turned 56 yesterday. Sent in my application today to the State University of New York's Empire State College. The Center for Distance Learning offers credit for life experience and independent study for people like me, who can't attend regular classes. Not sure what I'll major in. Not art. Maybe history.*

> *June 11: Went to Kingston to sign up for unemployment. The line was a real mixed bag of humanity. Felt awkward, but the staff was patient and helpful. The thought of going for job interviews depresses me. But the thought of never working again depresses me even more.*

> *Oct 5: Linda went to New Paltz to see Mose Allison in concert. I just couldn't bring myself to go. I don't feel like being with people. Hate to answer those "How's it going?" questions.*

> *Jan. 29, 1997: Sometimes I just want to walk out of the house and keep going. I feel extraneous. Despite all my interests and enthusiasms, I guess I still buy into that notion of man as breadwinner. I can intellectually deal with not contributing income to the family, but emotionally it's another matter. It gnaws at me.*

Aug. 25: First day of school. Everybody seemed to know everybody else, except me.

May 21, 1998: It's cool to have classroom buddies. My teacher friends and professors have encouraged me to consider public education. They think I would have something to offer.

Jan 19, 1999: First day of school, at Truman Moon School in Middletown. I'm student-teaching kindergarten and first grade. Greg, the regular art teacher who will take me under his wing, briefed the kids on the color wheel and how it works. They are extremely cute. Greg handles these kids very well, and they behave with respect. It is important to set guidelines and stick to the rules. I can see a certain face has to be adopted.

Feb. 8: The kids don't listen to me. Well, a few do. The restrictions are tight. Against the wall, hats off, no getting up, noise to a minimum—teacher as cop. I don't really like it.

April 15: All goes well. The last two days have been great. Wrapping up the Chinese landscapes. It's amazing how fantastic some of the work is! Better than I could do.

Healing and Crisis Journals

> *Writing is a form of therapy.*
> —Graham Greene

In recent years, there has been a lot of commercial attention placed on this kind of journal—not only because they are financially profitable to publish. Store shelves feature blank breast cancer and grieving journals, and there's a movement afoot, I hear, to produce divorce journals. These are just a few of the crisis situations where a journal would provide comfort and healing opportunities; most of us can think of several other crises as well that would lend themselves to journal keeping. But you don't need a specially designed journal for writing through and about a crisis or illness. Any blank book will do.

Designating a specific blank book to a crisis can serve to help encapsulate the experience. Although a crisis always enters other areas of our lives, the specified journal, as a place to turn to vent or confess or be sorrowful, can be helpful. This is the place to detail every trial, every misstep, every anger, every memory, every forbidden thought.

The crucial thing to remember is that you are writing for yourself alone. This is important to feeling free and giving yourself permission to include the bad with the good—

and, it is important to add, the good with the bad. Many journal writers feel that they only turn to their journals when life looks bleak or when they are feeling depressed. And this is frequently the case, especially in crisis.

One of the ways to make a healing/crisis journal work for you is to assign yourself the task of writing something positive in each entry or at least once a week—a funny thing that happened to remind you that you still have a sense of humor, an appreciation of a beautiful crisp day, a fond memory of the person who you're grieving for or a kindness that someone has done you. Including the positive serves a dual purpose: it will buoy you up while you're writing and positive thoughts are healing in and of themselves. Too often, in the midst of crisis, we lose all sense of perspective. The healing journal can be a place where we recover some of that positive perspective as well as a place to turn to release sadness and anger.

Dream Journals

Dreams are necessary to life.
—Anaïs Nin

There are some people who remember their dreams easily—and frequently recount them in great detail—and many others who wish they could remember even a frag-

ment of their dreams. If you are already a dream remem-
berer, then writing your dreams down in a journal is a
way to both keep track of your dream life and investigate
possible meanings for your dreams.

If you have trouble remembering dreams, as I do, the
very act of starting a dream journal can help you in your
quest to remember. About twenty years ago, I was in
graduate school and had a roommate who would regale
me with her dreams every morning at breakfast. I was so
frustrated by the ease with which my roommate could
recall every syllable and encounter from her nighttime
adventures that I decided to dedicate a journal to my
dreams. I recently reread that journal and was surprised
how the sheer will to focus on recalling dreams had,
after a short while, brought them to my conscious mind
each morning.

If you want to foster dream remembering, place a journal
and a pen or pencil near your bed, and if you wake up
remembering bits and pieces of a dream, write them
down. On those mornings that you wake up and know
you have dreamed but can't remember any specifics of
the dream, try writing a page or two of whatever comes
to mind, even about your frustration with not being able
to remember the dream. After awhile, this focus on your
dream life should rekindle dream memories.

Another interesting technique for keeping a slightly different kind of dream journal is to write, just before going to sleep, the dream you would like to have. For some people, this kind of suggestion actually begins a dream process. And even if it doesn't, writing about a wished-for dream will definitely begin a fruitful journal entry.

Scrapbook Journals

This is a wonderful kind of journal for people who collect keepsakes or mementos and is especially conducive to writing for those who are visually oriented. Anything you paste in a journal is itself a prompt for writing. So if you save postcards or matchbooks or hotel brochures or menus, try pasting them in a journal and see where they take you. My friend Peter Jensen, a writer, once told me, "Journaling comes easily for me thanks to my scrapbooking instincts. Knowing that I don't have to write frees me to write. Clip a quote, a photo...paste it in...write a wee caption, and before you know it, you're saying a bit more." He also wrote this lovely description of his "Home Journal" created in scrapbook method:

> My journal, and ones like it, are keepsakes of the self, created with full knowledge that they may become hand-me-downs far more personal than scratched initials in a childhood bedstead (who was PJ again?) or

a chipped tea pot (was this my grandmother's, or great-grandmother's?).

I call my method a Home Journal. With a Home Journal, you know who it was. It was him. It was her. (It was me!) They were my family, and they lived, loved, sweated and cried. They made good cookies and casseroles—you know this because you now have the recipes. They listened to long-forgotten music called Ragtime and the bandstand concerts featuring one Sousa piece after another.

You know this because instead of searching for fragments (photos, old dishes, clothes, military discharge papers) scattered throughout garages and attics, you encounter them on page after page of a Home Journal—all the thoughts, clippings and discourses written, pasted, Scotch-taped, or tucked in one place.

A Home Journal can be a complete, chronological melange of every memory you don't know where to keep, but don't want to throw away either. It can be the things you did, and the things you want to do (prompts on books to read, music to find, trips to take). What you wish for may help define life almost as much as what you do—be it achievement or failure.

Here's how a Home Journal works in real life—my own.

77

Some time ago I abandoned traditional attempts at journal writing. It would seem natural for a writer to write a journal. Many do. More don't. After many years and many fitful rambles in half-full notebooks, I gave up on writing regularly about my emotional ups and downs, or the day to day events that make up most of my life.

Words on paper never offered a complete picture.

I began keeping a bound notebook (made of what the museum folks call "archival" paper) in the one place I spend time in thought and quiet attempts at organizing things. For me, that's a desk upstairs. For others, it might be a kitchen table or beside a favorite television room chair.

Sharp little scissors are always nearby. So is tape. And a pen, usually one that readily gives up glorious lines of black ink.

When I read something wonderful in a magazine, I clip it out and tuck it in my journal. A postcard from a traveling son? In it goes. The title of a music CD I hope to remember to buy? I jot the title and artist's name down. A poem I write at the beach? It has a home. The snapshots from a trip to Canada? Lick 'em and stick 'em old-fashioned photo "corners" work as well today as they did a century ago. A sketch I want to do in the back garden? Why not do it direct into the journal?

One by one the pages fill. Some seem mundane. Some
are eerie predictions of the future; not just things that I
buy, or actions I take that give me pleasure, but trends
in my life and those around me. When I feel life is not
much more than happenstance, I need only look in my
journal to discover how much I really do plan, scheme,
hope, dream.

Creative Ideas and Observation Journals

If you are interested in nourishing the creative side of
yourself, a separate journal for ideas, images, and observations can be very helpful. Many writers keep journals both
to record their personal journeys and to serve as store-
houses for future projects, as you've seen in the first part
of this book. I always set aside a section at the back of my
current journal where I note ideas for stories or overheard
conversations that intrigue me. For example, I was getting
off a train one day in a suburban New Jersey town and
next to the station there was a tree with a heart carved in
it. Within the heart were the words, "Abdul loves Wendy."
Of course I wrote it down, thinking where but in America
could one find such graffiti? I have yet to use it anywhere
but in my journal and now here, but I hope someday to
use it in an article or story. And even if I never use it again,
the very fact of having a place to write it down and actually recording it made me reflect upon that found piece of
contemporary Americana. I also write down my

Hungarian mother's wonderful malapropisms—she says "overlistened" for "overheard" and "standbys" for "bystanders" and just recently told me that "it isn't done until it's not over." Writing these down is one of my conscious acts of appreciating my mother, and I've also used many of them in stories.

Creative journal observations are useful to the professional and amateur alike—and just setting aside some pages for them can increase your creativity. A graphic designer I know keeps a drawing journal and has begun painting again as a result. A musician keeps fragments of musical themes that intrigue him and has just recently used some of these themes in a new piece of music written for a television show. A research scientist keeps a record of insights that he may someday pursue, and now he's thinking of writing a book for the layperson based on some of these ideas.

The Gratitude Journal

This kind of journal can be as simple and straightforward as a daily list of three things that you are grateful for and that bring joy into your life, or as complicated as a series of meditations on what gratitude means in your life. It doesn't matter whether you mingle these approaches, stay with one, or mix in gratitude pages with your all-purpose journal. The most important aspect of a gratitude journal is to get you to focus for a few moments on what there is in your life to cherish.

Writing about gratitude is a very effective way to rearrange your perception of your life and the world, especially if you are going through a period where you are, as Shakespeare once wrote, "on Fortune's cap not the very button." Centering your thoughts around what is positive can refocus you, lift your spirits, and, perhaps, lighten your burdens. It can also prompt you to say "thank you" to others, a reminder I find to be a major benefit of a gratitude journal.

Avocation Journals

There are as many types of journals as there are human activities. So if you are avid about anything—gardening, birding, diving, hiking, bicycling, spelunking, flea market shopping, attending Chicago Cubs games—you might want to dedicate a journal to recording experiences, progress, observations, and discoveries about your favorite avocation. Gardeners include planting schedules, results, notes for the next season. Scuba divers keep diving logs noting locations, depths, visibility, and what they saw and felt. Collectors keep notes about finds and desires, while hikers log in trails, views, heights, and experiences. There are many examples of such journals, but here is one entry and sketch from a birder's journal kept by Susan Roney Drennan, an eminent authority on birding and the recipient of the Bushnell Distinguished Birder Award. The entry shows how specific and detailed a specialized journal can be:

DATE: 30 *May 1999*

PLACE: *Jamaica Bay National Wildlife Refuge,*
New York City, NY

TIME: *11:00 a.m.*

DURATION OF OBSERVATION: *approximately 25 minutes*

OBSERVERS AND OPTICAL EQUIPMENT: *Susan Roney Drennan with 10 x 42 mm Leica binoculars, Kenn Kaufman with 8 x 42 mm Leica binoculars, Paul Meyer with 8 x 42 mm Zeiss binoculars. We also have with us a Questar Sky and Earth 60 mm spotting scope (telescope) with a 15 - 45x eyepiece, which we use throughout the sighting.*

WEATHER: *Excellent, pleasant, balmy, no sign of rain or storms, the sea is calm with no whitecaps in sight.*

TEMPERATURE: *68-74 degrees F (from National Weather Service)*

SKY COVER: *Blue skies, some featherlike high cirrus clouds—stayed wispy throughout the day —primarily sunny and clear—not over-cast at all*

WIND (DIRECTION AND VELOCITY): *Gentle breeze, wind from SSE at approximately 12 m.p.h.; this would be Force 3 on the Beaufort Scale (moves leaves and small twigs and extends a light flag).*

DISTANCE FROM BIRD: *No more than about 35 to 40 feet*

HABITAT: *Intertidal mud flats exposed at low tide rimmed by short rich sea grass, spartina, and sandy beach*

SPECIES: *Long-billed Dowitchers was what we conclude after our field study*

NUMBER, AGE, SEX: *Three birds in fresh, full-adult, breeding plumage. Since the male and female are alike in breeding plumage, we can't tell their sex. These birds are gregarious and feed and fly together.*

RELATIVE SIZE: *Chunky, plump wader, medium-sized (10 or 11 inches) shorebird with long, straight, heavy bill, distinct eyebrow, and handsome chestnut red-brown plumage. These birds are about the size of an American Woodcock. Imagine that sized body sitting on top of long, thin, scaled legs.*

VOCALIZATION: *We note that these birds actively call in flight. The sound is a high, thin, sharp, kee or keek, usually a single note but two* or three times they repeat it rapidly as a triple note. They vocalize also while feeding and preening but the sound is much thinner and "conversational" than in flight. These gregarious birds are quite "talkative."

BEHAVIOR: *Feeding in mud and shallow water by vertically probing with its long, snipe-like bill, with a rapid, jabbing motion a lot like a sewing machine while moving in one and then another direction. Sometimes while feeding it entirely submerges its head for a moment in deeper water. Since they are so actively feeding, they seemed relatively unaware of us observing them. Sometimes in the middle of feeding they rise in unison, wheel around and settle back down on the mud flat. During these short flights it is easy to see the white rump wedge and details of the tail and wings, which are otherwise held close to the body and not easy to see.*

OTHER COMMENTS: *These notes have been made directly from our collective observations in the field while observing these birds for nearly one-half hour. The accompanying field sketch has been made in the field. No field guides were consulted in the field and once consulted later these notes were not altered.*

DISTINGUISHING FIELD CHARACTERISTICS

1. HEAD AND NECK (FOREHEAD, CROWN, MEDIAN LINE): *Crown dark brown; lacks striping or median line on the crown of some other shorebirds; forehead has a "flat" look.*

superciliuim - distinct
pale eyebrow

crown - feathered deeper
brown

LORE

MANDIBLES
upper
lower
is long - maybe
to three inches
K slate gray
color

NAPE is
spotted

HINDNECK
spotted

FORENECK
densely spotted

MANTLE

mantle & scapulars
have narrow feather
edgings - deep rusty red
SCAPULARS

BREAST - sides
densely spotted

BELLY

center of
belly clear
unmarked

uniform brownish
red

FLANKS
barred

feathers

RUMP in flight
white wedge
shape extends
up the back
about middle

UNDERTAIL
COVERTS marked
by narrow bars
chevron like

legs, deep green/yellow
very long look

TAIL FEATHER
PATTERN

An IDEAL Field Sketch

SEDREYNAN
'80

2. EYE & LORES (SUPERCILIUM): *Supercilium pale and distinctive; lores are crossed by narrow, neat, dark brown line which extends for a short distance behind the eye.*

3. UPPER & LOWER MANDIBLES: *Both the upper and lower bills are dark and straight; the total length is about 3 inches long and the bills look snipe-like.*

4. LEGS & FEET: *For more than half of the time we've been looking at these birds the leg color has been obscured by the soft wet dirt and mud in which the birds are feeding. However, when we get good looks, the legs have a very long look and appear as deep green/yellow. When wet they appear slate gray. When dry more of a green/yellow hue is seen.*

5. UPPERPARTS (NAPE, BACK, RUMP, UPPER TAIL): *Feathers of the upperparts—mantle and scapulars—are dark-centered and have narrow dark rusty edges, some have narrow white tips and some have gray or rusty tips. Upper rump is white and wedge-shaped and extends from the barred tail up the back to almost its middle.*

6. UNDERPARTS (THROAT, BREAST, BELLY, SIDE, FLANKS): *All of the underparts are entirely and uniformly brownish or chestnut red. Foreneck and breast are densely spotted; sides and flanks are barred; center of the belly is clear and unmarked. The undertail coverts are marked by narrow bars, some are chevron like.*

7. RECTRICES (INNER, MIDDLE, OUTER TAIL FEATHERS, COLOR PATTERN, SHAPE): *Tail has a very long dark look, especially in flight when they were flying directly away. At rest the tail is obviously heavily barred with white and black bars alternating and at some angles there was a look of the barring being black and cinnamon. The narrow light bars (white/light) are less than half as wide as the dark bars. The dark bars are always broader and often looked twice as broad as the white ones.*

PART THREE

writing to find
the way in

*The individual point of view
is the only point of view from which one is
able to look at the world in its truth.*
—Ortega y Gasset

THE BLANK PAGE CAN BE INTIMIDATING FOR ANY WRITER, AND knowing where to start is often difficult. Even experienced journal writers get stuck at some point or another. Sometimes the words just flow; at others times, the urge to write is present, but the focus is unclear. But this doesn't mean you can't get started putting words on the page.

There are a number of very good ways to get unstuck and to start the writing juices flowing. You may find that when you use one of these jumping-off places or practices, you open up a number of areas you might like to pursue in more extensive entries.

KILLING THE INTERNAL EDITOR BY FREEWRITING

Freewriting allows you to write with no subject and no idea in mind. It is one of the most effective ways of getting in touch with what is actually going on deep within you because freewriting bypasses the conscious editor that resides so solidly in all of us. Ever since the second or third grade, or whenever it was that we first saw those red correction marks on a piece of our written work, we have been trained to think first and write next—and to stop along the way and make corrections as best we could.

By not stopping to think or correct or even to make sense

as you write, you have a much better chance of accessing your subconscious. Therefore even if you write down what you think is the wrong word, a word you didn't mean to write, *do not* cross it out and correct it. Just keep going. That seeming error is not necessarily an error at all; it may be the subconscious coming to the surface. If you have to, write the "correct" word or what you meant to say right after the "wrong" word. When you reread what you've written, you may find how much more there is to write about your supposed "errors."

I often begin journal-writing workshops and college-level writing classes with a freewriting exercise. Invariably, within ten minutes, even those participants or students who have always hated to write and are reluctant to begin find that they have something to say. What is more, you may find upon rereading your freewriting that your writing is much better than you thought it was. This is one result of dropping that infernally cranky internal editor who is always telling you that you're making a mistake or that you should stop and revise because you could have said it better and made it more "correct."

Much of our early education in writing has to do with getting it "right" rather than making it interesting, creative, or authentic. Establishing a clear flow from within is much more important in journal writing than refining your prose. You will have plenty of time later on to seize upon and develop those ideas that intrigue you or move you or that you feel can lead to deeper insight or creativity.

Brenda Ueland, in her classic book, *If You Want to Write: A Book About Art, Independence and Spirit*, points to her freewriting journal as a great resource:

> *I have kept such a slovenly, headlong, helter-skelter diary for many years. I have written in it, off and on, and sometimes in exact detail and as minutely and accurately as the Recording Angel. Horrible things (that I did not know about myself) are revealed in it but perhaps remarkable things too. It has been a great help to me. This is what it has done for me:*
>
> *It has shown me that writing is talking, thinking, on paper. And the more impulsive and immediate the writing the closer it is to the thinking, which it should be.*
>
> *It has made me like writing. For years it was the most boring, dreaded, and effortful thing to do—doubt-impeded, ego-inflated.*
>
> *It has shown me more and more what I am—what to discard in myself and what to respect and love.*

How to Freewrite

Get comfortable, set a timer for ten minutes, and then put your pen or pencil to paper and write. The trick is to cover the page with writing and not think about what you're writing. If you have nothing to say, then write down "I have nothing to say," or "This is a stupid exercise, why am I doing it." Keep going until the timer rings. You'll find that even if you have started out by complaining about having to write, within a few minutes you will have dropped the whining and be inside of your head and writing down ideas or feelings or thoughts that you were not in touch with when you started the exercise.

Freewriting with a Focus

You can also try freewriting with a focus. Let your gaze travel around your environment and choose an object or a person. It doesn't matter if it's the coffee cup in front of you, a favorite photograph, the light slanting in the window, the waitress resting her feet, or your best friend reading the newspaper. Let your gaze rest on what you've chosen for a few moments and then begin writing as detailed a description as you can manage. Move on from the description to any associations that arise.

You might try doing the same with an emotion such as:

ANGER

LOVE

FEAR

JOY

SADNESS

PLEASURE

GRIEF

RESENTMENT

CARING

EMBARRASSMENT

AROUSAL

Other Freewriting Ideas

WORD STIMULI Many of us have favorite quotes or passages scribbled in notebooks or tacked up on refrigerators or bulletin boards. Try copying one of these into your journal and freewrite about that.

Another way to use word stimuli is to open a book (novels and poetry work best) to any page and just put your finger down at a random place and read the sentence where it has landed. This is a completely serendipitous exercise, and as such, it will sometimes work and sometimes fail. But when it's successful, you will find that a random sentence can start you writing in a vein you never would have anticipated.

OVERHEARD CONVERSATIONS If you are in the habit, as I am, of picking up snatches of conversation heard in the supermarket or waiting in line at the bank or the movies, try writing down one of these conversations that intrigues you at the moment you hear it. Later you can transcribe it into your journal (if you were journal-less when you heard it) and freewrite about the overheard conversation.

VISUAL STIMULI The mind often leaps to imaginative heights at the sight of something beautiful or frightening. Images can trigger intense emotions as well. You might try opening an art book or photo book, or even focusing on a magazine advertisement, or gazing for awhile at an old family photo. Close your eyes for a moment to make sure you have the image in your mind's eye, and then open your eyes and begin to write whatever comes into your mind.

The Right Brain/Left Brain Collision

Words and images that don't inherently belong together can excite new ideas or emotions. Often the unexpected combination of a word and image can bring our left and right brains together and move us to new insights. There is a set of cards called "Oh" cards, available in stores carrying esoterica or on the Internet, that facilitate this process very well. The "Oh" cards are composed of two decks of cards, one with miniature paintings and one with words. The idea is to choose one from each deck while they are face down and then to turn over the two cards at the same time, juxtaposing the random word and image. For example, the image might be a mother and child and the word might be "fear," or the image might be a clown and the word "embarrass." The prompt for writing comes from trying to make a connection between the word and image as they relate to each other and to the viewer's emotional reactions.

Even without a set of cards, you can create your own left brain/right brain collision prompts by writing a series of ten or twenty evocative words on index cards. Try words that connote emotion or book or song titles. Choose one without looking at it, and then flip through a magazine or an art book and select an image. Flip over the word card under the image and begin to write.

WAKING DREAMS

Fantasies fuel our daily lives, whether we realize it or not. I often tell my literature students that they have English Major disease. They believe that their lives have a plot, with a beginning, a middle, and an end, and they often interpret current events as foreshadowings of future events, which they then fit into their life plots. In reality, we all have English Major disease, and it is one of the healthier diseases known to humankind. We tell our-selves stories about our lives that we'd like to see come true. A journal is an ideal place to tell yourself stories about yourself and to follow your fantasies.

To begin a waking dream entry, imagine yourself in a sit-uation, real or invented, that intrigues you. Describe the environment in detail and then move on to create an event. Let your imagination go, don't censor, and see where your fantasy takes you. You may be surprised at the secret desires or fears that emerge, but always remember that this exercise is not necessarily predictive. You are simply exploring parts of yourself and views of your world that you don't normally see. The vantage point isn't always pretty, like catching a glimpse of yourself from behind in a three-way mirror right after a Christmas eat-ing splurge, but it is guaranteed to be informative.

GOSSIPING WITH YOUR JOURNAL

Gossip is a time-honored practice. The very word con-jures the vision of two or more people, heads close together, gleefully sharing delicious and probably scan-dalous bits of information, true or not, about other peo-ple. Oscar Wilde knew this and approved when he wrote, "There is only one thing in the world worse than being talked about and that is not being talked about."

In our time, gossip has risen to new and headier heights—gossip abounds in the media, in newspapers and magazines (*People* magazine was started because the editors at Time-Life realized that the first section nearly everyone read in *Time* magazine was the "People" section), on television, and on the Internet—so you may feel that there is no need for a lesson in gossip. And you're right. You don't need a lesson in gossiping, but what you might like to have is a push toward gossiping in your journal. After all, much of what we do in journal writing is to speculate about ourselves, about others, about the world, and to record observations and insights.

For those of you who might be uncomfortable at first with the notion of freewriting, try making journal entries as though you were gossiping with a friend. You might even name the friend in your mind or on the page. "Guess who I saw. . ." "You'll never believe what I heard. . ." "Who does she think she is. . . " make for very good beginnings. What you may find is that these forays into gossiping about others within your journal lead to more interesting entries, causing you to reflect about yourself.

QUESTIONS AS JUMPING-OFF PLACES

Asking yourself a question, preferably an open-ended question rather than one with a yes or no answer, can be a simple and straightforward way to dive into your journal and may give rise to some of your best entries. Try answering some of the following open-ended questions in ten minutes of writing:

- HOW AM I FEELING RIGHT NOW?
- HOW OLD DO I FEEL TODAY AND WHY?
- WHY AM I TRYING TO WRITE?
- WHY DO I ALWAYS ————?
- HOW CAN I HEAL MY RELATIONSHIP WITH ————?
- WHY DON'T I WANT TO SEE————?
- WHAT MAKES ME FEEL SUCCESSFUL?
- WHAT MAKES ME FEEL LIKE A FAILURE?
- WHY ISN'T ————RESPONDING THE WAY I WANT?
- WHAT IS MY GOAL RIGHT NOW?
- WHAT'S THE BEST WAY TO ACHIEVE MY GOAL?
- WHAT DO I WANT MOST IN MY LIFE RIGHT NOW?
- WHAT AM I WILLING TO CHANGE ABOUT MYSELF?
- WHAT IS MY GREATEST STRENGTH?
- WHAT IS MY GREATEST WEAKNESS?
- WHAT AM I RELUCTANT TO SHARE?
- WHAT DO I REALLY WANT TO SAY TO————?
- WHAT TURNS ME ON?
- WHAT TURNS ME OFF?
- WHAT DO I REALLY WANT?
- WHEN AM I THE HAPPIEST?
- WHAT BRINGS TEARS TO MY EYES? A LUMP TO MY THROAT?
- WHO DO I THINK OTHERS SEE WHEN THEY LOOK AT ME?

List-making seems to be a universal human activity. We make shopping lists, to-do lists, reminder lists, party invitation lists, packing lists, New Year's resolution lists—in fact, a list of lists could go on endlessly. Since the basics of list-making are so familiar to us, this technique is readily available for use in your journal-writing practice. List-making journal writing can be as simple as writing "a daily list of five things you are grateful for" or "your three intentions for the day" and as complicated as creating a list for structuring and completing a large project. The likelihood is that you will eventually choose to make both kinds of lists in your journal because they serve different purposes.

The following examples form an incomplete guide to different kinds of journal list-making—you will doubtless come up with more of your own as you write.

Lists for Accomplishing Tasks

Most of us make lists to remind ourselves what we have to do and to impose some order on our activities. Some of us even add items to our lists after we've done them so that we have something else to cross off. Of course, those of us who do this are just trying to convince ourselves that we've accomplished a lot. But those later additions are usually the things we would have done anyway.

Quite a while ago, I read a small but powerful book by Alan Lakein called *How to Get Control of Your Time and Your Life,* and I learned one of to-do list-making's most valuable and effective rules. He suggests making three lists, the A list for the big projects, the most important things you have to do, the B list for the secondary items, and the C list for the least important items. He then suggests you throw away the B and C lists for those are the things that you will do anyway.

To make a list for accomplishing a task, maybe in a project journal, begin by creating A, B, and C lists and, as Lakein suggests, start with the A list. But don't throw away the other lists. If they're written in the journal, leave them there, and if you've written them on separate sheets of paper, tuck these into the back of your project journal for reference (you might want to tape an envelope into the back of the journal for these lists and for ideas jotted on scraps of paper).

Establish a separate journal section for the largest, most intimidating item on your A list. Then from that item, say, writing a family history, make a list of the component parts of the project. If it's a book you want to write, break it down into:

- RESEARCH
- WRITING

Then create a list that evolves from each one of these items:

RESEARCH

- FIND AND READ BOOKS ON THE TIME PERIOD TO BE COVERED
- LOOK AT GENEALOGY CHARTS
- TALK WITH FAMILY MEMBERS
- GATHER PHOTOGRAPHS, LETTERS, AND MEMENTOS
- MAKE A LIST OF CHARACTERS
- MAKE A MAP OF FAMILY MOVEMENTS

WRITING

- DESIGN AN OVERVIEW OR OUTLINE
- FLESH OUT THE OUTLINE, PART BY PART, WITH CHARACTERS AND MEMORIES
- DEVELOP CHARACTER SKETCHES INCORPORATING DETAILS
- JOT DOWN MEMORIES
- DEVELOP EACH MEMORY INTO A PARAGRAPH OR TWO WITH DETAILS
- INCORPORATE PHOTOGRAPHS AND LETTERS

As you can see, each item on each list gives rise to more lists, helping you break down what seems like an impossibly large task into its component parts. This list-making approach works for any large project that has you feeling overwhelmed or floundering for a place to begin: a big project at work, a job change, or even a confrontation with someone (more about that later).

Warning: Project list-making is not an end in itself, although, I admit, it can be tempting just to keep making lists. At some point you do get down to the smallest activities and have to act on them. But at that point, you can begin to use the journal to write about the activities.

Lists for Self-Discovery

This kind of list-making has more to do with writing quickly and accessing the subconscious than does the project-oriented list-making technique. If freewriting is reminiscent of the literary techniques called stream of consciousness and interior monologue, list-making for self-discovery has its roots in free association, but with a focus, if that's not an oxymoron.

In this kind of list-making, you set the focus and then write a very long list of what comes to mind as quickly as you can. This may be the process that Paul Simon used to create his song "50 Ways to Leave Your Lover," but obviously you don't have to rhyme, unless you feel the urge.

Early in my journal-writing workshops, I always ask the participants to write down a long list of their desires, numbering at least 50 or even 100. The assignment usually elicits groans at first—"How will I ever get to 50, let alone 100," "I really don't want all that much," or "I'm not a material person." Of course, this kind of list rarely winds up being a schedule of material desires, although a new car or new furniture or jewelry might appear.

What most people find is that by being asked to write without thinking too much, they come up at first with things they know they want, then some things that seem like nonsense, and after a while, desires that surprise them will appear. I have to admit that sometimes factors outside of our internal urges, such as the environment, will dictate some of the items on the list. When I conduct a workshop at a spa, it's not unusual for chocolate or ice cream to show up early on a list. But even the yen for calories cannot take over this list-making process. Just as you might complain at first in freewriting about having nothing to say, that complaint soon gives way to what is really on your mind. The same is true of list-making— even if you have immediate desires such as cookies and milk, chocolate cake and ice cream, you will move past them on the list fairly quickly.

Once, when I had quite a few older women in a workshop, the big surprise for them was that many items on their lists of desires were not things they desired for themselves but rather desires they had for others, their children or grandchildren. In a way, especially for women, it is too easy to shift the focus away from the self in this manner. I asked these women to undertake a slightly more focused assignment and write another list that was filled only with what they desired for themselves. This was much harder for a number of them because they confused being selfish with having desires for themselves. Be wary of this trap in the list of desires practice.

I have no doubt that you can come up with a variety of lists you might want to make, but it always helps to be prompted. The following is an alphabetized list of 52 list topics.[1] If you decide to use this list, you might even choose to write one list each week, which means that these suggestions will take you through one year. Once you've decided on the list to write, set a writing time of 15 minutes and write as fast as you can without reflecting on each item. Don't worry if you repeat items.

1. AMBITIONS I HAVE
2. AMBITIONS I'D LIKE TO HAVE

[1] Some of these list suggestions come from Kathleen Adams's book *Journal to the Self: Twenty-two Paths to Personal Growth*.

3. BASIC ASSUMPTIONS I MAKE

4. BATTLES I'VE FOUGHT

5. CARING PEOPLE

6. CHILDISH PLEASURES I STILL DELIGHT IN

7. DESIRES THAT I HAVE

8. DREAMS THAT I HAVE

9. EXCUSES I MAKE

10. FEARS I HAVE

11. FAVORITE TURN-ONS

12. GOALS I'D LIKE TO SET

13. HEALTH ISSUES

14. INJUSTICES I'D LIKE TO SEE RIGHTED

15. JUDGMENTS I MAKE

16. KNOWLEDGE I'D LIKE TO HAVE

17. LESSONS I'VE LEARNED

18. MISSIONS I'D LIKE TO UNDERTAKE

19. MEMORIES I LOVE TO REVISIT

20. MONEY ISSUES I STRUGGLE WITH

21. OBSESSIONS

22. PEOPLE I MISS AND WHY

23. PEOPLE I LOVE AND WHY

24. QUESTIONS I'D LIKE ANSWERED

25. RESPONSIBILITIES I'D LIKE TO AVOID

26. REASONS TO MAKE CHANGES

27. SENSUOUS PLEASURES

28. SMELLS FROM CHILDHOOD

29. TASKS THAT NEED DOING

30. THINGS I'D NEVER TELL MY PARENTS

31. THINGS I'D LIKE TO TELL MY PARENTS

32. THINGS THAT ARE RIGHT ABOUT ME

33. THINGS I'M GRATEFUL FOR

34. THINGS THAT ARE GOING WELL

35. THINGS I'M GOOD AT

36. THINGS I'D DO IF I HAD THE TIME

37. THINGS I WANT IN A PARTNER

38. THINGS I'M GLAD I'VE DONE

39. THINGS I'LL NEVER DO AGAIN

40. TRAITS I'D LIKE TO HAVE

41. THINGS I'D LIKE SOMEONE TO TELL ME

42. THINGS I'VE ACCOMPLISHED

43. THINGS I WANT TO ACCOMPLISH

44. THINGS I BELIEVE IN

45. UPLIFTING MOMENTS TO BE THANKFUL FOR

46. UNRESOLVED ISSUES

47. VOWS I'LL NEVER BREAK

48. VOWS I'VE BROKEN

49. WAYS I AVOID DEALING WITH MYSELF

50. WISHES

51. WORK PROJECTS

52. ZEALOUS BELIEFS

You have probably figured out by now that list-making in itself is interesting, even fascinating, but that it is not necessarily an end in itself. Some of the list items that pour out will invariably be items you would like to investigate further. Often, if you review a list after you have finished writing it, you will find that a theme emerges. For example, if you are listing unresolved issues and there are a number of quarrels with friends on your list, you might want to devote a journal entry to exploring the way you deal with your friendships. Or take one of the things that is right about you and explore that further. Or take a work project and create a progress journal for it. Or take a memory and describe it in detail.

Just recently I made a list of ways that I was avoiding myself. It isn't the longest list I've ever made, but it certainly made me look at my behavior:

> *Ways I Avoid Myself*
> 1. *Constant noise at home—radio, TV*
> 2. *Driving with the radio on*
> 3. *Using phone calls rather than introspection*
> 5. *Logging on to the Internet*
> 6. *Avoiding my journal*
> 7. *Avoiding meditation*
> 8. *Reluctance to set goals*

9. *Overloading myself with work and deadlines*
10. *Shopping*
11. *Communicating more with others than with myself*
12. *Not spending enough time alone and with myself rather than with videos or busywork*
13. *Avoiding sad feelings*
14. *Avoiding all of my feelings*
15. *Making too many plans*
16. *Moving with such great speed*

These may sound familiar to many of you, and that is perfectly reasonable because I believe indulging in distractions and thereby avoiding ourselves is endemic in the modern world. After making this list, I immediately made one about ways to get in touch with myself, and then another one about the kinds of self-realizations or doubts that I was avoiding. And then I wrote a journal entry about my self-doubts. Most often a list gives birth to other lists—and to journal entries.

The list-making practice can also help you to access themes you may not have consciously considered. For example, items that appear on a list of things we are grateful for are frequently items that we take for granted and don't often think about, but when we write the list quickly, they appear unbidden. Making ourselves conscious about those things which we accept but do not acknowledge or treasure enough can be a rewarding experience both for journal writers and, eventually, for those around them.

A Positive Caveat

The idea is to get the pencil moving quickly.
—*Bernard Malamud*

In making lists of desires, journal writers often notice that once put down on paper, many of these desires materialize. One of my journal workshop participants came back the year after making a list of desires and told me that she and her husband had refound their desire lists several months after writing them and were amazed at how many of their desires had come true. I have noticed the same phenomenon, and I don't think this is the result of magical thinking. Rather, I believe that once you write what you want, spontaneously and from the heart, the likelihood that you will get it is much stronger because by writing it down, you have acknowledged the desire. Once acknowledged concretely, in writing, the desire goes from being vague to being an item on a long-term "to-do" list. Even if you don't get to it immediately, it is there to be acted upon or received.

*What lies behind us and what lies before us are
small matters compared to what lies within us.*
—*Ralph Waldo Emerson*

It may seem that all I have been discussing are encounters with the self. And since, for the most part, that is what journal writing leads you to, it's true. But now I would like to explore specific practices that take you deeper into your own mind and subconscious. It is a good idea to be comfortable with writing quickly by now, because spontaneous writing will come into play in the next practices as well.

Everyone who uses dialogues in journals owes a debt to Dr. Ira Progoff, whose book, *At a Journal Workshop: Writing to Access the Power of the Unconscious and Evoke Creative Ability*, details five types of dialogues—with persons; with works; with the body; with events, situations, and circumstances; and with society. His system is complex and extensive and will benefit anyone who makes the commitment to studying it.

But you can also begin a dialogue journal practice immediately, often with profound results, by following the practices outlined below.

Dialogue with Your Body

> *A writer's mind seems to be situated partly in*
> *the solar plexus and partly in the head.*
> —*Ethel Wilson*

Since I often teach journal writing at spas, body image is a frequent topic. Over the years, I have come to realize that many of us complain or even rant about our bodies, out loud or to ourselves, but we don't often investigate the consequences of our complaints. Getting in touch with how our dissatisfactions affect our behavior can be the first step in doing something about our complaints. I have seen many women write dialogues with their thighs or noses and men with their balding heads or pot bellies and come out with more insight into themselves and more compassion for their bodies. The following practice can work wonders.

STEP ONE Draw a stick figure of yourself but greatly exaggerate the part of your body you are most dissatisfied with. If you hate your nose, draw a Pinocchio nose. Or if you feel that your belly is out of proportion to your body, extend it in the way you imagine it looks, distorting reality. Or, if you are having a problem with pain in your joints, as did one workshop journal writer, emphasize every joint on your body, maybe even drawing radiating arrows emanating from knees, knuckles, elbows, and ankles.

STEP TWO Look at your drawing for at least thirty seconds. Then, close your eyes for one minute and concentrate on the part of your body you exaggerated in the drawing. Really focus on that part of your body and allow all of your feelings about it to surface. When you open your eyes, start to write a dialogue between you and your body part.

Here's a dialogue I recently had with my belly, which I have always felt is too big:

> *Me: I can't believe it, I've worked so hard to get rid of you and here you still are.*
>
> *Belly: Get used to it—I'm part of you and you can't deny me.*
>
> *Me: Sure I can—I can wear loose clothes, suck in my gut, obliterate you with Pilates exercises.*
>
> *Belly: Why can't you just accept the fact that you're a woman and women have rounded stomachs—what's wrong with you—is this about getting old?*
>
> *Me: Not really—it's about perfection—struggling with it still at this late point—why the hell can't I just relax and enjoy the body I have.*

Belly: Start with me, please—I'm so sick of being to blame for whatever problems you have.

Me: I don't blame you alone—really—a lot of the time I lump you with other flaws, like my thighs are beginning to go.

Belly: Wait a minute, what happened to acceptance — remember that book you once read about logotherapy—exaggerating a flaw or fear so it won't seem so overwhelming.

Me: Right—maybe I should just eat myself into oblivion.

Belly: Now you sound like a child—get your act together, or I won't even cooperate about letting you suck me in.

Me: Okay, okay—this swinging back and forth is about dealing with external perfectionism—it probably keeps me from getting past you to the things I really need to feed myself with.

Belly: That's a great place to start, but you're pretty glib. I'd think more about that if I were you.

Clearly my belly had a lot to say and so will whatever part of your body you choose to start a dialogue with. I must say I was surprised by both the intelligence and feistiness of my belly—even though I can assure you that

I know my belly doesn't really have a mind or voice of its own. It is one part of my own intelligence, but one I don't usually listen to.

Journal writers are often surprised by the results of this exercise. Take the workshop participant who suffered from rheumatoid arthritis and set out to write a dialogue with her painful joints. She wrote for ten minutes and then reread her dialogue. What amazed her and the rest of the group with whom she shared her surprise was that although she fully intended to write a dialogue, she never got to it. She began her writing by ranting and raving at the joints, which were causing her so much pain and limiting her activity, and she went on for so long that she never gave her joints a chance to speak. She realized that the entry was a microcosm of her battle with the arthritis. She had been complaining and fighting with and against the pain for so long that she wasn't listening to what her body had to say at all. This writing practice encouraged her to begin an ongoing, emotionally and somewhat physically healing dialogue with her body.

Breaking out of a habitual complaint cycle and getting away from focusing only on dissatisfaction and pain can allow your deeper knowledge to surface. This is a productive way to gain new and rewarding insights into a repetitive and perhaps destructive pattern.

Dialogue With an Undesignated Part of Yourself
For this practice you don't have to start with a dialogue partner defined. Rather you begin with a question, any question, something that's been on your mind or one that just pops up as you sit quietly for a moment. I like this practice because it almost always accesses responses that are unexpected, coming from deep within the subconscious. Frequently, you'll find that after several exchanges in the dialogue, you will be able to identify your dialogue partner—but don't worry if you can't. The process will still give you valuable information.

Sometimes as we write the dialogue it becomes obvious that the other voice is an inner critic, or a rebellious child, or a buttinsky mother, or any number of the other voices we carry within ourselves. Some of the more frequent partners in these dialogues are easily named parts of the self, such as:

- THE INTERNAL CRITIC
- THE FRAGILE EGO
- BOSS MAN OR LADY
- EVERYBODY'S HELPER
- MS. MAKE EVERYTHING ALL RIGHT
- THE SELF EXCUSER
- MR. IN CHARGE

Starting the Internal Dialogue

Sit quietly and clear your mind. It's best to do this in a place with no immediate distractions or noises. Breathe deeply, calming your mind and body, for a full minute. Then allow your mind to bring up questions that might be of concern to you at the moment. As soon as a fully formed question comes into your mind, open your eyes and write it down. (If you're feeling frustrated because you're not coming up with a question, don't despair, you can still try this practice. Just begin with "Why don't I have any questions right now?")

Now this is the most important part of this exercise: Don't think, just write down an immediate response to the first question.

Continue the dialogue in this manner—writing quickly for one speaker and then the next until you come to a natural stopping place, either when something that you've been writing about is resolved or when you run dry. Don't worry if the dialogue doesn't seem to make that much sense, and don't worry if you can't immediately identify the other speaker. After a few exchanges, you will probably begin to recognize the respondent. And if not then, you certainly will upon rereading the dialogue. Don't be surprised if the unnamed voice expresses a kind of clarity or insight that your conscious

voice cannot bring forth. This kind of dialoguing can reach deep into your subconscious, enabling you to emerge with previously hidden or unacknowledged information.

At the beginning of a journal-writing workshop a few years ago, I sat down and wrote the following dialogue with an unnamed part of myself:

> Me: *Why do I fear this not going well when I've done it so many times?*
>
> X: *There's always a first time for failure.*
>
> Me: *Oh come on—do I really have that much of a chance of failing?*
>
> X: *That's better, now you're being feisty rather than insecure.*
>
> Me: *This insecurity has plagued me for long enough—it's time to get rid of it but now it only comes up when something means a lot*
>
> X: *You've just answered that yourself—who cares if it doesn't count*
>
> Me: *Now that's the question—what makes something count for me?*

X: You've been struggling with wanting something to count for a while now—after all your list was full of that

Me: You're right—is this about commitment?

X: Sort of—it's about whatever you want it to be

Me: Don't back out now—you've been giving advice—don't turn into a reflective therapist

X: Okay, making things count—you do practice living in the moment fairly often—it's when you get away from that that the insecurity comes up—every moment needs to work that way for you.

It turns out that I truly needed that advice and that prompt to stay in the moment, and for the rest of the week I practiced it. This dialogue resulted in one of the best weeks and workshops I have ever had.

ELABORATING MEMORIES

> *We are stricken by memory sometimes,*
> *and old affections rush back on us as vivid as*
> *in the time when they were our daily talk.*
> —William Makepeace Thackeray

Memories of the past, often unbidden, flit across our minds at random moments. Sometimes there's something going on in the present that triggers a memory—a speaker reminds you of your second-grade teacher or the taste of a food, or the smell of perfume brings back another time and place. Capturing these memories on the page can enrich your sense of yourself and your own history. Writing about the memory in detail can enable you to probe deeper into what it is about that moment that makes it important or memorable to you.

You can write about memories in a variety of ways—by focusing on a specific image that comes to mind unsought or by focusing on a time in your life that you'd like to explore further.

Here's a memory piece I wrote beginning with a recollection of my childhood experience of the smells in our kitchen. Although the entry begins with the concrete, it quickly moves to the emotional realm:

6/12/97

It's that smell. First the acrid, tart uncooked sharpness, then the slowly mellowing, slightly sweet cooking aroma. My mouth is watering but in anticipation of what? I don't even like fried onion on top of my potatoes. That was my father's favorite. But that smell is the signal that he is coming home, that I would take my school books off the table, that dinner would replace them. My mother, bustling in the kitchen, worrying the utensils—"are they sharp?" "where is the grapefruit knife?" "Oh, no, I forget, did I put salt in already or not? Mamele, did you see?"

I didn't. I never do. The kitchen is her world with its meat and diary dishes, it's speckled green linoleum that is so clean you could eat off it, the water running endlessly over the chicken splayed on wooden slats for koshering. The kitchen is the old world and I'm in the new—the dinette just 6 feet away but another world. I'm in America she is in a small town in the Carpathian mountains doing exactly what her mother had done. Even at 7, I know that I will never do that.

Writing memories is a rewarding practice for people of all ages, whether they have a lifetime of experiences to sift through or just two decades or less. Whether you're writing about childhood, early adulthood, or a more recent memory, you are still time-traveling to an earlier version of who you are now. Going back and recreating a moment or a series of moments can reintroduce you to a time in your life and remind you of who you were then. At the same time, you are recapturing the past, both as evidence and experience.

Recently the *New York Times* ran a feature story about a new trend in senior citizens' life story journal-writing groups. Sara Rimer wrote, "These new memoirists are writing for the same reasons writers have always written: to search for meaning in their lives, to find their voice, to leave a record." Although I might disagree with the term "memoirist" for these journal writers, for the memoir writing comes after the spontaneous journal writing is done, the reasons for writing about memory are valid for journal writers and memoirists alike. Capturing detailed memories in your journal is certainly a large part of finding the way in.

Memory Practices

1. Sit comfortably with your eyes closed, and let your mind roam. Let memory images arise, without judging or choosing at first. Then focus on a particular memory image that intrigues you, either because it is fresh and vivid or because you'd like to recall more of it. Build on the image, fill in the details of sounds, sights, smells, textures, voices, characters. When you have it set in your mind, open your eyes, and write as fully and completely as you can about that memory.

2. Deliberately choose a memory to focus on. Some good starting places are:

- SITTING IN THE KITCHEN AS A CHILD
- LEARNING TO DANCE
- MAKING A FRIEND

- SITTING IN YOUR CHILDHOOD ROOM
- THE FIRST DAY OF SCHOOL
- THE FIRST DAY OF A NEW JOB
- ENCOUNTERS WITH RELIGION
- FALLING IN LOVE
- FIRST KISSES
- EMBARRASSING MOMENTS
- FEELING WRONGED
- CHILDHOOD CRIMES
- THE DEATH OF A PET
- EARLY HIDEAWAYS
- FIRST COMMUNION
- SHOPPING FOR NEW CLOTHES
- FIRST FUNERAL

First anythings are very good for memory writing because they stand out in our minds. "I remember the first time I . . ." is the opening of many a story told by father to son or grandmother to granddaughter. And everybody's firsts are different, so don't fear writing clichés just because there may be thousands of people writing about a first kiss. No one had the same kiss as you did. So write the memories until they bring the sounds, sights, and tastes of the moment to life. And write freely—if you're going to turn the journal into a memoir, you will have to revise it (more about this later), so for now just get it down in as much detail as you can.

3. Write a long list beginning with "I remember" and then choose specific items to explore in depth. This list can be used as an ongoing prompt list for a memory journal. You might even paste it into the front of a new journal dedicated to memories.

4. Begin a journal entry with the words "I remember" and freewrite from there.

Building a Journal of Memories

For anyone interested in writing autobiographically, devoting a specific journal to capturing memories is a good practice. You might start with the memory list mentioned above, or you might decide to use a more chronological method by creating a timeline of your life.

The timeline can be constructed according to dates or events or both. Most of us can divide our earlier lives into preschool, grammar or elementary school, high school, and perhaps higher education. Summer memories are usually distinct from schooltime memories, and summer houses, camp experiences, family vacations, or part-time jobs form some of our most intense memories.

1. Try writing about a summer memory, perhaps including the beach paraphernalia you used as a child—buckets, plastic shovels, and water wings—or the time at the lake when you thought your best friend was going to drown.

2. Try making a chronological list of schools, and maybe even grades and specific teachers you remember. I always find that character sketches of teachers bring to mind specific memories of myself in those classrooms.

You don't have to make memory entries in chronological order, but it is helpful to make a rough timeline, say through the course of a blank journal, and then begin to write the memories that are strongest at any particular moment in the present.

3. Another technique for prompting yourself in memory writing is to consider where you were when specific world events occurred. Depending on your age, you will have distinct memories of the deaths of certain world leaders. My parents tell vivid stories of being on the streets of New York when they heard that Franklin Delano Roosevelt died. All of my contemporaries know exactly where they were and what they felt and did when they heard that John F. Kennedy had been assassinated, that the *Challenger* spacecraft exploded, or that Ronald Reagan was shot by John Hinckley. Try taking a world event that affected you personally and write about that memory.

4. The most intense memories are those concerned with our personal histories—marriages, births, deaths, and the many triumphs and losses that go into making up our individual autobiographies. Choose among these memories and write about them in your private timeline journal.

5. Using specific prompts to remember moments in the past can be useful in unblocking memories. One of my favorites comes from a birthday party a friend of mine threw for herself several years ago. She asked all of her friends to come dressed as the people they thought they would grow up to be when they were ten. There I was, done up as Rita Hayworth, surrounded by a ballet dancer, a priest, a wrestler, and a chef.

If you want to spur a childhood memory entry, try reflecting back on your childhood fantasies, hopes, fears, and dreams. Write about them first from a child's point of view and then move on to your adult point of view.

6. Try drawing a favorite place from your past. It could be your childhood room, a playroom, a schoolyard, an ice-skating rink, a tree house, or a clubhouse. Whatever still remains visually vivid in your mind's eye can be sketched on the page. Afterward, fill in the memory with words as you write a journal entry about the place you've drawn.

Using the Senses

Engaging the senses for writing is a powerful tool for evoking memories that we often can't put into words. Smells are our first sensual reactions as babies, and most people can recall how as children they could recognize their mother's pillow from their father's by the smell. An aroma can send you back looking for specifics, both visual and emotional. An aunt's favorite perfume or a first lover's cologne, inhaled in the present, can bring back the details of momentary encounters or even of long periods in your life. The smell of Ozone hairspray, which is no longer produced, or something very much like it, reduces me to a fifteen-year-old teenager in my best friend's bedroom where we are preparing ourselves for a Friday-night party.

So engage more of your senses for writing. If there is an aroma that sends you back, use it to ease yourself into a memory for writing. The same goes for a piece of music or a favorite song. Play it, and write.

GETTING UNSTUCK:
CHANGING YOUR POINT OF VIEW

One of the frequent pieces of advice given to fiction writers when they get stuck with plot or character development is to change the point of view they're using. So if you have begun to write a story in the first person and run dry, the idea is to try writing in the third person—instead of writing "I" write "he" or "she." This shifts the writer from the internal to the external and can provide new insights into the character or situation. The reverse is also true—shifting from "he" or "she" to "I" gives the writer a new perspective and can break writer's block.

The same technique works very well for journal writers, almost all of whom write in the first person. If you've gotten weary of all that "I think," "I feel," "I want," try switching to "he feels," "she thinks." Writing about yourself in the third person can be both liberating and enlightening. Just by switching pronouns, you are forced to see yourself from the outside, a perspective we don't often get on ourselves. The very act of distancing yourself from the character, "the I," you are writing about, enables you to have a clearer view. In this mode, you can also gain a better perspective of how your thoughts and actions fit into a larger world.

You may also find that if you are someone who is prone to making judgments about yourself, they sound much harsher when you are writing about yourself in the third person.

- THIS IS A GOOD PRACTICE FOR PEOPLE WHO ARE TRYING TO BE KINDER TO THEMSELVES.
- THIS IS ALSO AN ESPECIALLY GOOD PRACTICE FOR PEOPLE

If you are having trouble writing about yourself in the third person, another option for achieving the same end is to write about yourself as though you were writing from the point of view of a good friend. In that way, you are not dividing yourself in two, but rather creating the voice of someone you know well who is describing you and commenting on your behavior.

ENCOUNTERS WITH OTHERS

A journal is an ideal place to deal with your emotions and thoughts about other people and

- TO BEGIN TO HEAL RELATIONSHIPS
- TO VENT FEELINGS
- TO EXPRESS EMOTIONS AND THOUGHTS THAT YOU
  FEAR STATING IN PERSON
- TO WORK OUT PROBLEMS
- TO SAY THE FORBIDDEN
- TO TRY OUT NEW FEELINGS AND APPROACHES

In many situations, a journal can function as the so-called "dry run" for real encounters. Doing this in private writing can defuse some of your fears. Once articulated on the page, your words or thoughts are made concrete, and then you can revise or edit, if you like. You may find that the process of writing out planned interactions removes the heightened and emotionally obsessive quality that can occur if you tend to rehearse or review interactions in your mind over and over again. This practice can be useful with past interactions as well.

Dialogue With Another Person

This dialogue-writing practice is very much like the ones described above, except that it feels more familiar. You begin by choosing to conduct a conversation with some-one you know. You don't have to know the person well, or it can be someone with whom you have a close or intimate relationship. You are the one who begins the dialogue with a question or a statement, and then you quickly write the other person's response.

The most important part of this practice is to let the other person speak. This may require ceding a certain amount of control to another's point of view. Remember, this is a dialogue. You may be surprised how much empathy you have for the other person's point of view and how much you can learn from this practice.

Unsent Letters

The idea of an unsent letter is something many of us are familiar with either in our minds or in action. Who hasn't had the impulse to tell someone off in the strongest words possible? Or to write the love letter that might put too much on the table too soon or too late? Or the confession that might be inappropriate? Or the apology that we feel might put us at a disadvantage?

In the unsent letter practice you have the chance to write freely exactly what you feel, and you are the only speaker. You can say what you like—rant, rave, grovel, plead, confess, admit—and you don't have to worry about a reader.

Of course, there are times when you might want to send the letter you write, but never do this immediately after writing it. Sometimes the exhilaration of finally getting our feelings out impels us to action—but this can be impulsive and potentially unwise. Wait a day or two and reread the letter. Then, if it says exactly what you still want to say, or if you can revise it to say what you want to say, transfer it onto your stationery and send it out. Unsent letters can be useful:

- TO VENT ANGER
- TO APOLOGIZE
- TO SPEAK OF LOVE
- TO SAY THANK YOU
- TO CONFESS
- TO PLEAD

Letters to the Dead

I recently heard a story about a man standing by the grave of his wife, sobbing. The priest waited nearby and after a while came to the man and said, "It's time to go." The man, still sobbing, said, "I loved her so much," whereupon the priest said, "I know, my son, but you have to let go now." The bereaved man said, "But I loved her so much, I loved her so much, and once, once, I almost told her."

Of course, the lesson here is to speak of love while those we love are alive, but how often, upon hearing of the death of someone you knew, have you said or thought "I wish I'd told him/her —————." In an unsent letter to the dead, you have an opportunity to express those feelings and say the words you didn't say. This kind of unsent letter can be used for grieving and healing as well as venting. Writing a letter to the dead is often immensely therapeutic and can also provide a kind of closure.

A few years ago, one of my colleagues died. I missed him enormously. But it wasn't until six months after his death when I sat down and wrote a letter to him telling him what he meant to me and why I missed him so much that I was able to deal with my grief. The letter gave me the chance to remember specific moments and conversations that brought him vividly back for a few moments. My unsent letter also served another very valuable purpose, for it was the basis for a letter I wrote to his widow about how loved he was by all of us who worked with him for many years.

It can also be comforting to write a series of unsent letters to someone who has died who was very important in your life. A friend of mine died in a car accident several years ago. Her daughter, who was then nine, was seriously injured in the same accident. Now she is fourteen and has been writing a series of letters to her mother for the past two years. She knows very well that her mother is dead and will never read these letters, but in writing them she keeps the memory of her mother alive and vital. This series of letters also functions as her journal.

CHARACTER STUDIES

Capturing someone's personality through language is an intriguing way to take a closer look at how you view another person. The very act of finding adjectives and creating a verbal snapshot forces you to envision the person in a more complete manner. It's also possible that in the struggle to find words, you'll discover how lopsided, skewed, or incomplete your view of the person might be. Magazine profile writers often pepper their articles with a subject's personal gestures, verbal tics, style of dress, and physical attitude. Try employing some of these tactics for creating character sketches of people you know.

Two experiments:

1. Write a straightforward character description of someone with whom you have either a good or bad relationship, trying to be as visually and emotionally evocative as you can.

2. Write a completely exaggerated description of the same person using the devices of caricature such as distorting one particular characteristic.

Which one is easier to write? Which comes more naturally? Have you realized anything about your own possible prejudices? Your intolerances? Your need to pigeonhole?

Another way to do a character study would be to avoid physical description altogether and simply present the character in terms of his or her language, emotions, attitudes and others' reactions to him/her. Try doing this with one of your character studies.

WRITING IN ANOTHER'S VOICE

This kind of private writing has a lot in common with writing about yourself in the third person and dialoguing with someone else, but in this practice you put yourself in someone's mind and write from his or her point of view. It might seem at first thought to require too much empathy or even telepathy to do such a thing, but once you begin to write, you'll find that it isn't difficult to establish the voice of another person, and you begin to identify his or her point of view fairly quickly.

It is especially useful to choose to write in someone else's voice when you are having difficulty understanding why that person has behaved or is behaving in a way that is frustrating or confusing to you. This could be true of a co-worker, family member, or lover. Try to quiet your own mind first and imagine yourself in that person's metaphorical shoes. What is he or she looking at? Thinking? Feeling? You are seeing the world through the other person's eyes, and the "I" in your writing becomes his or her voice.

You may feel awkward at first, but keep writing. After awhile, you will set aside your own indignant voice and begin to identify with the other person's point of view. This is an especially healing writing practice to try after you've had an argument with someone, since at these times most of us are so caught up in our own sense of black and white and right and wrong that we tend to forget that other people can think and feel differently than we do.

Discussing description brings up rather naturally the idea of drawing in a journal. Artists keep sketch pads with them, and I know they make notes underneath or along-side drawings at times. And many journal writers make drawings in the midst of words. As one journal writer told me, "I also sketch a lot, which—for me—is the ultimate way in. Writing is hand-mind, sketching is hand-eye-mind…a full circle of both body and mind." This man happens to be a professional writer who finds that draw-ing frees up the part of his editorial self that too often and too intrusively begins to judge his private writing.

There are any number of reasons to use drawing in your journal—to remember a particular object that you would have difficulty describing, to draw a memory that you want to write about such as a childhood room or toy, to feel the sheer joy of the pencil moving across the page in a nonwriterly way. Drawing can be freeing, whether or not you have any talent for it.

Try drawing in your journal at some point, either to cap-ture something seen or to make visible something unseen. Don't worry about your art skills or how repre-sentative the image appears to be. Try drawing slowly, and then try drawing in the same way you make a list—as quickly as you can. See how it feels to let the pen or pencil travel over the page. See what it brings up. See whether it works for you.

ENCOUNTERS WITH THE FUTURE

> *The future enters into us, in order to transform itself in us,*
> *long before it happens.*
> —*Rainer Maria Rilke*

If one of the most dreaded questions for you is "Where do you want to be in five years?," this might be a good exercise. Personally, I hate to plan for the long term, and I have always felt this way. The idea of going to a job interview and having to answer a question about my long-term goals fills me with dread. I'm not even good at planning vacations too far in advance. The future just seems so amorphous, and there is a large part of me that enjoys a sense of mystery about the unknown. After all, anything can happen. But I have come to realize that I do have goals, even if I resist acknowledging them, and I have learned that recognizing them can help me reach them. Journal writing has helped—partially due to list-making and especially due to writing future entries.

If you, too, are a bit future-phobic, writing future entries can help you come to terms with goals.

Living in the Future Perfect

1. Write a date sometime in the future at the top of the page—try one dated six months from now, a year from now, and five years from now. Or try writing an entry dated on your next birthday.

2. Close your eyes for one minute and visualize yourself on the date you've selected. If it is now May 12th and you're writing an entry for January 15th of the next year, set the scene by imagining the weather and where you might be sitting on that date.

3. Open your eyes and write the date and place first. Begin to write about how you are feeling and what you are thinking. Where are you? What have you done that day? Who have you spent time with recently? What is making you particularly happy? Sad? What have you accomplished? What are you looking forward to accomplishing?

One of the truly rewarding aspects of this exercise is to look forward, past a current conundrum or emotional situation and see where you will be when you've solved the issue. Sometimes this exercise actually can provide you with the tools or approaches to solving current problems.

ENCOUNTERS WITH THE CREATIVE IMAGINATION

> *Imagination is more important than knowledge.*
> *—Albert Einstein*

In the first part of this book, I included some excerpts from a variety of journals, some by writers, as well as quotes from various writers who talk about how they use their journals either to store material for creative work or to prompt creative work. If you are a writer, or an aspiring writer, your journal can be the place where you try on ideas, images, writing styles, characters, and plots.

The Idea Album

> *I don't write in my journal daily or habitually.*
> *I limit it to notions and images I can't live without,*
> *which are mostly concerned with germinating work.*
> *—Jim Harrison*

Many writers and composers and artists jot down ideas as they occur. Some put them in books, others use a catchall receptacle—an old cigar box or envelope—and still others are amazed at finding these scraps of paper in their wallets and pockets months or years after they've been written. If you are someone who is thinking about saving ideas, anecdotes, character sketches, or overheard conversations, you might want to give some thought to how and where to keep them.

If you carry your journal with you, you might want to set aside a section, maybe in the back, for creative ideas. If you are the kind of person who jots down ideas on scraps of paper, why not paste an envelope into the back of your journal and put those scraps in it to be looked at when you have the time to write more. In this way, you'll be keeping a collection of creative prompts.

The more serious you become about creative writing, the more you might want to dedicate a specific journal to these endeavors. Then you won't have to scramble through your all-purpose journal to find the creative idea nuggets you've stored.

Free Association Lists
Free association lists are a wonderful way for a writer to access ideas from the subconscious. In his book *Zen in the Art of Writing*, Ray Bradbury says:

> But along through those years I began to make lists of titles, to put down long lines of nouns. These lists were the provocations, finally that caused my better stuff to

surface. I was feeling my way toward something honest,
hidden under the trapdoor on the top of my skull.

The list ran something like this:
THE LAKE. THE NIGHT. THE CRICKETS.
THE RAVINE. THE ATTIC. THE BASEMENT. THE
TRAPDOOR. THE BABY. THE CROWD. THE NIGHT
TRAIN. THE FOG HORN. THE SCYTHE. THE CAR-
NIVAL. THE CAROUSEL. THE DWARF. THE MIRROR
MAZE. THE SKELETON.

I was beginning to see a pattern in the list, in these
words that I had simply flung forth on paper, trusting
my subconscious to give bread, as it were, to the birds.

Try making your own free association list for a scene or
event that you might want to turn into fiction.

The Walk-Through Poem

> *To a poet nothing can be useless.*
> *—Samuel Johnson*

Another way to use a list in writing creative work, poetry particularly, is a technique I call the walk-through
poem method. You can do this by accessing a memory or
actually being in a place and taking notes. The technique
is simple. You basically chart your movements—body,

eye, and mind—through a place or event, until you come to a logical stopping point. In a way, you are making a small story about a moment in time.

You might want to try a dry run for this practice by walking around your house or apartment. Write down each move you make very straightforwardly, for example,

I open the door to my study,
The desk is piled high with unanswered mail,
Too much for me to deal with today
I close the door softly
Not wanting to awaken my guilt

You probably won't produce a poem you want to keep during your first stroll, but finished work is not the object of this exercise. Rather, it's a warm-up to get you writing and to uncover some ideas you might want to play with in the future.

A walk-through poem can also capture immediate feelings and impressions that you might not be able to write down more elaborately in a tense or difficult moment. You may even find that its required succinctness elicits an emotional shorthand that can be quite powerful. Here's a walk-through poem I wrote right after visiting the Holocaust memorial at Yad Vashem, Israel.

Yad Veshem

Stones, black sculpture
Black hearts
Grainy large pored
Mementos of German scrapbooks
Scrap heaps
Names, camp names
Names from our past
Auschwitz, Buchenwald
Treblinka, Bergen Belsen
Names from current nightmares
In the past a communal reality
Names, a hall of names
A photograph of a fresh young man
From Budapest, murdered
In Auschwitz
An eternal flame under
An oppressive stone ceiling
A flame sending shadows and light
On a map of never ending pain

The walk-through technique can also be particularly fruitful when applied to past events and memories where it can unearth unbidden and powerful images.

Try doing one of the memory exercises and drawing a map or floor plan of the space you are remembering. Then record the memory as a walk-through poem.

Once again, I returned to a memory of my mother's kitchen for this still rough walk-through poem:

I'm standing in the kitchen where
my mother is sitting, beating egg whites.
She's using a beat-up spoon
in a battered old pot.
Her effort makes the egg whites rise
and I'm waiting to fold
them into my bowl
which is full of the mixed up
flour and sugar and egg yolks and nuts.
I look at the oven.
She warns me to stay clear
It's hot.
She stands and pours the stiff and frothy whites
slowly into my bowl as I fold the layers of batter
into the whites.
I reach under the sink for the square pan
and hold it out, waiting for her to pour the finished batter.
I carry it so carefully to the oven
and wait again for my mother's signal,
the moment for setting it down.

I feel the heat rising,
my eyes burn and tear
but I don't let her know.
It's my job to place the cake in the oven
the last stop before it's done.
Yet I stay in the kitchen, waiting
waiting for the signs, the heat, the smells.
My mother moves to get the candles to light
and places them carefully in the candle sticks.
I watch her every move, knowing
that she will cover her face
before lighting them, and then lift
her hands revealing tears.
She looks at me and remembers her mother
who died in the ovens.

Keeping a Character's Journal

Fiction writers of many stripes invent journals for their characters—from André Gide to Martha Cooley—and the actress Jennifer Jason Leigh keeps a journal from the point of view of every character she plays on screen. I am sure this is not a practice confined to people with the last name Leigh, but I believe Vivian Leigh did the same thing for her character when she playing Blanche Du Bois on Broadway in *A Streetcar Named Desire*. In fact, I think the director Elia Kazan suggested the technique to her.

One of the best ways of getting inside a character's head, or developing a character, is to keep a journal for him or her. So, if you are a fiction writer, a playwright, or an actor (or are aspiring to be any of these), you might try dedicating some journal pages to writing from a character's point of view. In this way you develop the character's voice, tastes, opinions, quirks, etc. You can even detail what he/she wore, ate, thought during a particular day and how the character thought other people reacted to him/her. A character journal is also a good place to invent dialogues between the character and others, or to recall the character's early memories.

Some of this material may find its way into the work of fiction and some may remain background that you can refer to when you construct how a character will behave in a certain situation. The journal will help you find the way into the character's mind and soul. No matter how you eventually use it, the material in a character's journal will inform and deepen the character in your fictional work.

MINING YOUR JOURNALS
FOR MEMOIR MATERIAL

You may find that writing in a journal liberates memories that you have not recalled before or that you have not had access to before. A private journal is one of the safest places to explore all kinds of memories. At some point, if you are interested in writing for a larger audience, you may want to take some of your memories and use them in writing projects. But for the most part, what you've written in the journal is not usually crafted the way a piece for an external audience would be.

T. S. Eliot wrote that the only way to express emotion in the form of art is by finding an "objective correlative"—a series of objects or a situation or a chain of events—that provokes in the reader the same emotion the artist wants to communicate. In other words, if you have expressed a great emotion in your journal and want to express it in a piece for an external audience, you can do this most effectively not by simply telling about the emotion but by creating an environment in which the reader can experience the emotion for him or herself. I believe this is a fundamental truth in writing for a reader. Some writing teachers sum it up by saying "Show me, don't tell me."

Entire books can be, and have been, written about what makes for good writing and good reading, and it is essential that the private journal writer not be thinking about a reader or feeling the pressure of good writing while making journal entries. That would defeat the purpose of keeping a journal.

Yet, if you do want to write for a reader eventually, you might start with some journal entries and try to create something that a reader reads not as an eavesdropper but as a fully-engaged participant.

You may remember the memory entry I included earlier, about the onions cooking in my childhood kitchen. I took a bit of that and tried to turn it into the beginning of a memoir, still in the first person, but more as a storyteller, including dialogue and creating an ending. It's not finished, but it shows you how a memory can move closer to a piece meant for an external reader.

> My mother worked very hard to have me, or at least that's the story she's always told me, usually in the kitchen, and often when she's cutting onions, maybe so the tears won't go to waste. "Five years, I tried, you don't know," she begins, and then comes the part about the doctors—"We went to see a big man, a very big man, in the field, who finally helped." The pregnancy is usually glossed over, probably in order that she can move more quickly to the long hours of labor—"Oy, how I suffered, such pain you should never know"— followed by the Caesarean section—"And then, they cut me"—all made worthwhile by my arrival—"But look, mamascheine, all of it was worth it because it's you I have." Between the Hungarian rolled "r"s and the

old world syntax, the tale is delivered with the lilting cadence of a Yiddish Zsa Zsa Gabor.

This is usually followed by the story of my name. My father's sister, my Aunt Terry, had a baby daughter named Rita, and my mother fell so in love with her that she wanted her own Rita. And, five years later, when I was born, she got her. I didn't find out until many years later how pissed off Terry was. Imagine, there you are with your lovely little five-year-old Rita and suddenly your sister-in-law ups and names her baby Rita. And two houses away, no less. So I became Baby Rita and, you guessed it, my cousin was Big Rita.

But there's another story to my name, more important even than the one I made up in elementary school about how my pregnant mother had gone to a Rita Hayworth movie and just knew her daughter would be a movie star. And there's another story to why my mother wanted me so badly. It's the real story. It begins with my mother's mother, it ends with Auschwitz, and it begins again with me.

For every bit of journal writing, or any kind of writing for that matter, that you want to turn into a piece for a reader, you have to consider two issues:

- THE AUDIENCE
- YOUR OBJECTIVES

These considerations are precisely what you do not pay attention to when you are making journal entries, although you will find that some of your journal entries will work in a memoir as well. But when writing for a reader, you will have to fill in certain contexts that you may know intimately but to which you cannot expect the reader to have easy access. Those associations that come immediately to your mind when discussing your mother have to be filled in. The same goes for information about your family structure, the time and environment in which you lived, the social circumstances of your family, and the motivations for actions that might seem as plain as day to you, but which become obscure without appropriate background information.

If you want to write for a reader, your journals are ideal raw material. But in writing a journal you have been, for the most part, trying to suppress the self-conscious editor. Transforming journal writing into memoir writing requires paying conscious attention to crafting and refining a story. Once you place the notions of audience and objectives into your writing mind, though, you can take the self and memories you have revealed in your journal and apply yourself to the memoir writer's task.

Envoi

I hope throughout the preceding pages you have found many invitations to keep a journal and perhaps even reasons to write more frequently than you might have expected. There is no trick to journal writing and all of us have the wherewithal to keep journals.

All of the practices, suggestions, and exercises in this book are made for repeated use because both the processes and resulting writings are based upon who you are and how you feel at the precise moment you are writing. Therefore, none of these approaches to writing ever gets old or used up. There is an unending self within you to be fathomed, explored, and revisited time and again in your journal. The writing suggestions included in these pages are just the beginning. I know that as you write you will discover many more as you continue to find the way in.

RECOMMENDED READING

Adams, Kathleen. *Journal to the Self: 22 Paths to Personal Growth*. New York: Warner Books, 1990.

Baldwin, Christina. *One to One*. New York: M. Evans and Company, 1991.

————. *Life's Companion: Journal Writing as a Spiritual Quest*. New York: Bantam Books, 1991.

Bender, Sheila, ed. *The Writer's Journal: 40 Contemporary Writers and Their Journals*. New York: Delta, 1997

Bradbury, Ray. *Zen in the Art of Writing*. New York: Bantam Books, 1992.

Capaccione, Lucia, Ph.D. *The Creative Journal*. New York: Newcastle Publishing, 1989.

Cerwinske, Laura. *Writing as a Healing Art*. New York: Perigee, 1999.

Chapman, Joyce. *Journaling for Joy*. New York: Newcastle Publishing, 1991.

Cooley, Martha. *The Archivist*. New York: Little, Brown, 1998.

Fitzgerald, F. Scott. *The Crack-Up*. New York: New Directions, 1956.

Frank, Anne. *The Diary of a Young Girl*. New York: Bantam Books, 1991.

Goldberg, Natalie. *Writing Down the Bones*. Boston: Shambhala Press, 1986.

————. *Wild Mind*. New York: Bantam Books, 1990.

Hagan, Kay Leigh. *Internal Affairs A Journal Keeping Workbook for Self-Intimacy*. New York: Harper San Francisco, 1990.

Hughes, Elaine Farris. *Writing from the Self*. New York: HarperCollins, 1991.

Mallon, Thomas. *A Book of One's Own: People and Their Diaries*. New York: Ticknor and Fields, 1984.

Metzger, Deena. *Writing for Your Life*. San Francisco: Harper San Francisco, 1992.

Rainer, Tristine. *The New Diary*. New York: Jeremy Tarcher/Perigree, 1978.

Payn, Graham, and Sheridan Morley, eds. *The Noël Coward Diaries*. Boston: Little, Brown, 1982.

Porte, Joel, ed. *Emerson in His Journals*. Cambridge, Mass.: Belknap Press of Harvard University Press, 1982.

Progoff, Ira. *At a Journal Workshop*. Los Angeles: Jeremy Tarcher, 1992.

Saroyan, Aram. *Last Rites: The Death of William Saroyan*. New York: Morrow, 1982.

Sarton, May. *Journal of a Solitude*. New York: W.W. Norton, 1977.

Schiwy, Marlene A. *A Voice of Her Own*. New York: Fireside Books, Simon & Schuster, 1996.

Thoreau, Henry David. *Walden and Resistance to Civil Government: Authoritative Texts, Thoreau's Journal, Reviews and Essays in Criticism*. Edited by William Rossi and Owen Thomas. New York: W.W. Norton, 1992.

Ueland, Brenda. *If You Want to Write*. St. Paul, Minn.: Graywolf Press, 1987.

Wakefield, Dan. *The Story of Your Life: Writing a Spiritual Autobiography*. Boston: Beacon Press, 1990.

Woolf, Virginia. *The Diary of Virginia Woolf*. Vol. 4. San Diego: Harcourt Brace, 1982.

INDEX

Jensen, Peter, 76–79
Johnson, Samuel, 63, 142
Journal of Solitude, 35
Journals:
avocation, 81–87
character sketches in, 24, 26, 134–35
choosing book for, 50–52
creative ideas and observation, 79–80
daily life recorded in, 18–22, 23–24, 25, 31–37
dating entries in, 53–56
destroying, 54
dialogue practice in, 112–20
diaries vs., 15, 16, 45–46
drawing, 80
drawings included in, 113–14, 127, 137–38
dream, 74–76
elaborating memories in, 120–28
encounters with creative imagination in, 140–47
encounters with future in, 138–39
in fictional works, 29–31
for fictional characters, 146–47
freewriting in, 91–96
gossip in, 20, 27–29, 98–99
gratitude, 80–81
healing, 73–74
health benefits of, 10
keeping everything in, 53
kinds of, 11, 62–87
lists in, 101–11
memoirs vs., 46–49

mining for memoir material, 124, 147–51
myths about, exploded, 11
no taboos in, 56–58
other people's, reading, 15–16
perceptions and musings in, 20, 23, 79–80
places for writing in, 61–62
planning and progress, 67–69, 102
privacy of, 58–61
questions as jumping-off places in, 99–100
reluctance to start writing in, 9–11
scrapbook, 76–79
self exploration in, 22, 32–37, 39–41, 56–58, 104–11, 112–20
sharing with others, 60
special event, 66–67
thinking out loud in, 25
time for writing in, 20, 61–62
in times of crisis, 37–40, 73–74
tradition of, 15–41
transition, 70–72
travel, 56, 63–66
urge to write in, 10
waking dreams in, 97–98
walk-through poems in, 142–46
writing in another's voice in, 135–36
writing on computer, 52
as young girls' confidants, 16–19, 38–40

RITA D. JACOBS, Ph.D., is a journalist and college professor who, for the past ten years, has been conducting workshops and classes on journal writing. In addition to her course offerings at Montclair State University in New Jersey, Jacobs has taught at such exclusive resort spas as Rancho la Puerta in Baja, Mexico, and The Golden Door near San Diego, California. She is a contributing editor to *Spafinder* magazine and has written for the *New York Times, Parade, Self,* and *Glamour,* among other publications. She resides in New York City and Woodstock, New York.